# TRACES OF MY FATHER

# TRACES OF MY FATHER

## SIGFRID GAUCH

**Translated from the German by William Radice
and with a preface by Antony Copley**

NORTHWESTERN UNIVERSITY PRESS
EVANSTON, ILLINOIS

Hydra Books
Northwestern University Press
Evanston, Illinois 60208-4210

Originally published in German under the title *Vaterspuren*. Copyright © 1996
Brandes & Aspel Verlag GmbH, Frankfurt am Main, Germany. English transla-
tion copyright © 2002 by Northwestern University Press. Published 2002 by
Hydra Books/Northwestern University Press. All rights reserved.

Printed in the United States of America

10 9 8 7 6 5 4 3 2 1

ISBN 0-8101-1890-4

**Library of Congress Cataloging-in-Publication Data**

Gauch, Sigfrid.
[Vaterspuren. English]
Traces of my father / Sigfrid Gauch ; translated from the German by William
Radice and with a preface by Antony Copley.
p. cm.
ISBN 0-8101-1890-4 (alk. paper)
I. Radice, William, 1951– II. Title.
PT2667.A77 V3813 2002
833'.914—dc21
2002003988

## FATHER ALMIGHTY

*Fish on concrete:*
*The air he earlier took from us*
*And for which we begged*
*I would give him it a thousandfold!*
*His refusal, called emphysema.*
*Himself a doctor.*
*With the fingers*
*That he earlier pushed back*
*The air caressed above him*
*That he clutches*
*("Should I become a child killer?").*
*I him.*
*What he needs: can't be wished for.*
*Father as in a synonym.*
*To cut the cord: to be able to talk about that.*
*To remain tied: to have to stay silent on that.*

*On through the streets*
*Wind in hair*
*Unbridged.*
*Bitterness not only in grimaces.*
*To lie there with never the air*
*For survival:*
*Fish on concrete;*
*Himself a doctor.*

# Contents

# HITLER'S CHILDREN
## A Preface to Sigfrid Gauch's
### *Vaterspuren*

Sigfrid Gauch's memoir of his father touches on all the major themes of twentieth-century German history prior to reunification. Here is the story of an elder generation that fought in the Great War, shared in the rise of Nazism, sold out to the criminality of the Nazis in power, contrived to survive the denazification process and to go on to contribute to postwar German recovery; here is the story of a younger generation that endured the anguish of a childhood blighted by the secretiveness of parents unable to confront their past, and that dealt with this repressiveness by the revolt of 1968. The younger generation was belatedly to break the silence that such a childhood imposed, and increasingly we have a literature, a genre in its own right, interpreting this experience. The commentary of the children on their parents has always been one of the more surreal aspects of all those endless documentaries on the leaders of the Third Reich: the seemingly normal offspring of the monstrously abnormal. In a somewhat scary, symbiotic way these children are beginning to match their parents as a kind of specialized elite. The Israeli psychologist Dan Bar-On even inspired in 1985 the setting up of a kind of psychotherapeutic self-help group for such children, Martin Bormann its best-known name. Not that the children have any reaction in common. Gudrun Himmler remains an unrepentant defender of her father. Martin

Bormann converted to Catholicism and worked through his guilt as a priest. Some have sought to exorcise the burden of being their father's offspring in corrosive rage. It is difficult, however, not to become alienated by the anger and overheated prose of Niklas Frank's study of his father, Hans Frank, the governor-general of Poland. It makes a difference whether the children were born early enough to experience the Third Reich, and Gitta Sereny felt—she was writing in 1967—that these were always the children most likely to insist on the truth being told about their parents.

Sigfrid Gauch, however, was born in 1945, and though he counts as the first to break the silence, he was to do so only after his father's death. His method is elliptical. This is no sustained analysis, simply memories, almost at random, prompted seemingly by the three days he spent organizing his father's funeral. He writes in a dry, laconic way, with a kind of detachment that draws one into the horrors he describes far more effectively than does Niklas Frank's angry prose. In some ways this is a teasing account and we need to know far more about his father. It is never clear whether we encounter a figure almost in the front rank of the Nazi move-ment or an also-ran. In what sense was he a typical Nazi? We have to fill in as best we may on the son's narrative—though he has since provided further information—and try to piece together Herman Gauch's links with the leadership, with Himmler, Walther Darré, Alfred Rosenberg. More seriously, we have to gauge the extent of his contribution to its murderous ideology. The poss-ibility of a misguided idealism, leading him into the movement at an early stage, has to be offset against the contribution that he made to race theory. We can but speculate whether the father was directly responsible for murder, but the culpability of the theorists cannot be underestimated.

It has been suggested that the chronic, historically specific context of the father-son relationships of Hitler's children places them in a different category from the usual Oedipal father-son conflict. Only accounts from other backgrounds could effectively put that claim to the test. Clearly, through writing this memoir,

Sigfrid Gauch is himself as much under review as his father. The text reveals that, unusually, the father did talk about his past with the son until there came a time when they had to go their separate ways—though toward the end the past was once again opened up. This limited degree of truthfulness almost certainly contributed to a diminution of the guilt that other sons had to endure through the secretiveness of their fathers. The son contrived to love the father but hate his ideas. But how did Sigfrid Gauch learn to cope with the burden of being the son of a Nazi?

## The Life of Herman Gauch

The one pleasing continuity in his life was his roots in the Rhineland-Palatinate. He was born in the village of Einöllen on 9 October 1899, was to be buried there in November 1978, and much of his life was to be spent as a doctor in the neighboring town of Kaiserslautern. Did this rural background influence his quasi-mystical views on the virtues of the peasantry? Little is revealed of his own parents, though here is offered the only rational explanation for his anti-Semitism: his father, a farmer who worked abroad to supplement his income, was, or so it is claimed, at some stage swindled by Jewish financiers in Amsterdam over a deal to do with diamond mines in Africa, impoverishing the family. He was but fourteen years old when his father died of malaria in East Africa. Was he ever afterward looking for alternative father figures? He was educated in 1913 to 1917 in Kaiserslautern and Augsburg. Now he begins to fit a Nazi stereotype, volunteering for the army in March 1917; joining the Royal Bavarian infantry, to be seriously injured at the battle of Soissons on 18 July 1918; imprisoned (after capture by the Americans) in a French POW camp in Blaye in the Gironde, though it was to be easy enough, in 1919, to make his escape.

Postwar, the young Herman led parallel lives, on the one hand training as a doctor, on the other pursuing his proto-Nazi career. In July 1924 he qualified in Munich as a doctor, in 1929 he acquired a certificate as state doctor: he was to be a doctor in the merchant marine and later the state marine, 1927 to 1933. While working in hospitals in Kiel and Wilhelmshaven, he acquired specific qualifications in psychiatric and nervous diseases, hygiene, and bacteriology. On 3 November 1922 he signed on with the party in Munich, a Nazi of the first hour, still too green to recognize Hitler's leading confidant, Dietrich Eckart, but the first encounter with Hitler in December proved fatal: "He looked me so directly in the eye that I felt quite peculiar." In a group photograph of Rudolf Hess's SA unit, Gauch stares out, the one unsmiling face. Together with his brother, Karl, he was involved in the assassination of the president of Rheinland-Pfalz, Heinz-Orbis, but, as was always to be the case with Gauch, he escaped the consequences of his political acts: he was condemned in absentia by the French authorities to five years of imprisonment for terrorism. He now restricted himself to his writings. His was an idealization of a pre-Roman Saxon peasantry, with a collective ownership of the land. His taxonomy of race appeared as *New Foundations for Racial Research,* to be published in 1934. It was for ideas such as these that he was picked up by Walther Darré in Kiel in 1933 and transferred to the Nazi party headquarters in Berlin. Here he met Hitler again and was again transfixed by his gaze. As he later informed the German historian Walter Maser in April 1976, "When Hitler for the first time gave me his hand and looked me so directly in the eye, I believed that he objected to my uniform . . . (I was wearing the marine uniform). But then I realized that he always and with everyone looked in that way."

It was not at all surprising that Gauch should have gravitated into the cliques surrounding Darré, Himmler, and Rosenberg. Argentine-born Walther Darré, partly educated at King's School, Wimbledon, was both a perfectly sensible land economist and a crank with mystic ideas on the peasantry and race, published in *The Farming Community as the Life Source of the Nordic Community* (1928) and *New Nobility from Blood and Soil* (1930), ideas which echoed Himmler's own. On the strength of this, from January

1932, he ran the Race Office, studying ways of recruitment for the new SS elite. Darré offered Gauch the post of director of his Ethnology Department. Himmler had taken up agriculture in frustration at not finding any military career and had already arrived at a weird vision of an original Aryan community living on the land but poisoned over time by interbreeding forced on them by Jews, Jesuits, and Freemasons. He nursed a fantasy of German settlers in the east, *Lebensraum,* taking their Aryan wives with them. The Estonian German Alfred Rosenberg had arrived in Munich in 1919, bearing memories of the Russian revolution in Moscow, and was to turn himself into the party's leading theorist. He had hopes that his *Myth of the Twentieth Century* would be for the movement what H. S. Chamberlain's *The Foundations of the Nineteenth Century* had been for an earlier anti-Semitic generation. Rosenberg also looked back to a medieval peasant past, to the heroism of a Saxon king, Henry I, slayer of the Slavs, and had even found a proto-Nazi hero in the medieval mystic Meister Eckart. As much anti-Christian as anti-Semite, Rosenberg also delighted in conspiracy theories of a combined Catholic, Jewish, and Freemason plot against the Aryan race.

It seemed as if Gauch had opened up for himself the prospect of considerable advancement within the Nazi regime. He rubbed shoulders with other rising stars, Heydrich and Eichmann, and was a close friend of Oswald Pohl, the director of the concentration camps and later of the death camps. Pohl was his superior in the Reichsmarine in 1933 and they shared neopagan beliefs. In 1934 Gauch's book on the ancient German constitution was named as one of the "six books of the month" by the *Reichsschrifttumskammer* (Reich Literature Panel), and the possibility arose of a professorship in peasant ethnology in the Department of Agriculture at the University of Berlin. But in the end funds were not forthcoming. Gauch had hoped to fashion a new peasant aristocracy, views he handed on tirelessly to Darré, Rosenberg, Himmler, even Hitler. But all his hopes had collapsed by 1935. What went wrong? In the absence of any guidance from the son's text, we are obliged to speculate. Maybe in the vicious infighting within the Nazi elite Gauch had chosen two losers. If Darré held on to his post as Minister of Agriculture till 1942, he had earlier fallen out with Himmler. If Rosenberg had once been seen fit to replace Hitler as leader during his imprisonment, he was never to reach such heights again and had struggled even to get the office of so-called Director of Indoctrination after the seizure of power. Possibly Gauch felt ill at ease with the compromises made with capital and the German establishment during the period of the consolidation of power; but in fact the Night of the Long Knives signaled the rise of the SS and the beginnings of a new phase of ultrarevolution. There was no longer any need to court the peasant vote. Additional recent information provided by the son is crucial here. He sees his father as an extremist, fanatically committed to a wholly German, non-Christian state and disaffected by the seeming compromises of the Nazi party in power. He had, for example, radical proposals on restructuring the calendar according to his pagan beliefs. But one suspects temperamental factors were just as important. Possibly Gauch was just too quarrelsome, too disappointed in his ambitions, too much the loner, and in the end a marginal figure. Still, he became a *Gauleiter,* or local boss, in Kaiserslautern, and became active in the Reich Labor Service. Once again he took up his medical practice.

But history is catching up with Gauch, and the Federal Archives in Berlin fill in more of the gaps. By early 1937 his role in the Reich Labor Service was under attack. It seems that someone had reported him for views on the Catholic Church deemed incompatible with the party line. What we do not know. Was he taking a more extreme line than the official, still cautious policy on sterilization? A Dr. Schröder wrote to him on 2 February 1937, expressing personal faith in him but telling him all the same to look elsewhere for employment. Gauch fell back on a memorandum dated 13 October 1933 that stated that no National Socialist should be treated disadvantageously, complained that junior members of the Reich Labor Service had been promoted over him, denied any pro-Catholic opinions, demanded more than oral evidence against him, and finally resorted to the rhetoric of his having been a frontline soldier and a Nazi of the first hour. He had his defenders. A Dr. Wilhelm Kintelin thought Gauch was wholly reliable, found it quite dishonorable that he was threatened with being on the streets, and wanted to recruit him to a race research body, the *Ahnenerbe* (notoriously, it was later to study twins). But Gauch lost. Whether this threatened his practice as a doctor is not clear—the Reich Labor Service exercised a monopoly control of all employment—but it may explain his having the time to acquire an additional qualification in gynecology.

There was another struggle over party and SS membership. Gauch rejoined the party on 1 May 1934, and not only the party but the SS, indeed the SD, lynchpin of the Nazi police state. He had first joined the party in late 1922, but following its reestablishment in February 1925 (after the failed Putsch of 1923) had not reregistered because his career in the marine ruled out membership of any political party. In 1934 he was told that backdating his membership to 1925 was impossible—an early membership number would have brought greater privileges—and that he was lucky to have been enrolled at all in 1934, a time of massive recruitment. In February 1935 he resigned from the SS (though he remained a party member), and according to his son this was prompted by his refusal to marry—a new requisite for SS membership, following the scandalous exposure of homosexuality in the Roehm circle. Himmler was personally to turn down his request for readmission in March 1937. Gauch's failure to impress Himmler while his adjutant (for only four months) for cultural and race affairs probably does most to explain his failure to make headway as a Nazi.

It is difficult to know how original or influential Gauch was as an ideologue. Clearly he belonged to that tradition of hostility to industrialization and the city that so strongly informed the *Völkisch* movement. There is a case for seeing a kind of warped quasi-socialist idealism in the movement, and Gauch shared in that sentimental quest for class fraternity, anti-Semitism in one of its garbs being a response to the Marxist insistence on class conflict. The young Gauch wrote a story in which the Browns and the Reds linked up to challenge the French and the Rhineland separatists. His ideas on race derived from a romantic love of the Norse sagas: Darré even sent him on a trip to Iceland. But Erika Mann saw his textbook on race as a key one in the educational system, and it presented truly poisonous opinions: all the non-Nordic races were deemed the same as animals, and, to quote the book, "it has however not been proved that the non-Nordic man cannot be mated with apes." Crude ideas on eugenics were widespread in the aftermath of social Darwinism, but nowhere were they taken up with such terrifying literalism as in Nazi Germany.

However incriminating his record as a theorist, did Gauch go one step further and become a killer within the Holocaust? We know that he volunteered again at the outbreak of war, was invalided out of the Luftwaffe, and then served as a medical doctor in the Twenty-third Luftnachrichtenregiment, which was noncombatant. On 24 October 1942, he reapplied for membership of the SS—with Pohl writing a reference on his behalf—and was again turned down, on 27 November 1942, by Himmler. Whatever Gauch knew or did not know about the emerging Holocaust—and he must have been aware of the beginnings of genocide against both the Serbs and the Jews in Croatia where he served—he wanted to be part of it. He was still in touch with Rosenberg's office in 1943; he then became head of a hospital in Lauterecken. Between 19 November 1944 and 19 March 1945 he was on the western front, and was once again invalided out through serious injury. Did he ever serve on the eastern front? There is a mention of his belonging to the Seventeenth East Poland Regiment. He boasted that it was he who suggested to Himmler that the SS should bring Nordic-looking Polish children to Germany to be brought up as Nazis. Gitta Sereny sees the abduction of children from the east as one of the most wretched crimes of the Nazi state. After the war Gauch became an open Auschwitz denier, seeking to prove how impossible it would have been for the crematoria to have killed so many. He was branded a desk murderer at the Eichmann trial and lived in fear of assassination by Mossad thereafter. Was he responsible as a doctor for any acts of murder? He certainly sent one so-called sex deviant to a concentration camp in 1938. It is appalling enough that Gauch felt no shame at Nazi crimes against humanity.

Postwar, once again Gauch got off lightly. A recent inmate of the camps, a denazification judge named Ludwig Moses, recalled Gauch's career in the 1920s and sought his detention, but died too soon to press charges. The French did issue a warrant for his arrest. But Gauch sought sanctuary in the British zone, known to be the most lenient, and in 1949 he was to be cleared by the denazification committee, admitting only to being a member of the National Socialist Doctors League—all he could fit in, he told his son, on the relevant line of the form. The committee decided he had never held office, proof in miniature of what a farce the denazification program proved to be. In early 1951 he sought Pohl's indemnification—he was then in Landsberg jail—from the death penalty. Gauch flirted with the far right and still entertained the idea that a neo-Nazi party could come to power and he would be its culture minister. Given his past he could not practice as a state doctor, but back in Einöllen he made a living in private practice, by all accounts quite a respected doctor, although prone to acts of black humor. He moved back to Kaiserslautern in 1962. He died an unrepentant Nazi. "This is the superego" Sigfrid Gauch writes, "with which I have to live." A case of guilt by proxy. How in fact has the son come to terms with the father?

## The Father-Son Relationship

Sigfrid's parents married in 1943. His mother was but seventeen, a member of the Organization of German Maidens, her youth a clue to his father's liking for young girls, a perversion that led to their separation seven years later. The son's account is curiously lacking in references to Herman's relationships with women— mother, wife, daughter, or the mistress he acquired after parting from his wife—and he has said subsequently that this was in large part to spare the sensibilities of his mother and sister. But the lack seems appropriate in describing a Nazi whose world saw a pathological search for manliness, the internalization of a pseudomasculinity. If the father is the role model and the means by which the son resolves identity, then in the case of Sigfrid, born on 9 March 1945, this problem was compounded by having an elderly father, forty-five years old at the time of his birth.

Unlike Niklas Frank, Sigfrid was spared the need to experience revulsion at a privileged lifestyle. He did, however, have to endure the way the Nazi generation in the postwar era, robbed of their self-esteem by defeat and the poisoned memories of their youth, turned to the family as a means of propping up their wounded pride. Behind that lay the even greater tyranny of the German tradition of "respectability." The parents in that era—always seen as enslaved to the economic miracle and siring a merely materialist culture—have possibly not been given their due for enduring the front line of the cold war and for looking outward into Europe. But to their children, even their best qualities could seem oppressive. The young Sigfrid had to suffer his father's constant if well-meaning presence in his education at nearby Meisenheim: "It wasn't until much later that I learned it was possible *not* to watch over one's sons like this." And there was a sinister side: his father tried to pass off his own poems as those of his children, in a pathetic search for some reflected glory. Yet in many ways the father did prove to be a role model. If being an officer was in the father's estimate the mark of being a man, the son became a lieutenant in the reserve. If becoming a schoolteacher for children with learning difficulties was a way of distancing himself from his father's career, it could be argued that becoming a senior official in the Ministry of Culture in the Rheinland-Pfalz was a paradoxical fulfilment of the cultural ambitions his father had entertained. More revealingly, the young Sigfrid had published when sixteen years of age a story in an anti-neo-Nazi journal, *Twen,* a piece about joining a kind of neo-Nazi youth group and listening to a lecture on race by a character clearly modeled on his father; and if the point of the story was to show how he had seen through the pathetic nature of all that, it revealed, nonetheless, that his father's Nazi opinions had made a transient mark. Blind to such ambiguities, Herman's only response to the story was to say of the fee that it earned, "*Qui mange du juif y mort*" ("Who eats by means of the Jew dies"). Ever the anti-Semite, he assumed that any left-wing journal had to be Jewish.

The means whereby the son could come to terms with his father, could continue to love him while despising his career and ideas, was to discover the pathos and frailty underlying all his posturing. He was not a brave soldier. He was always a shirker. He never stuck to any one task. "You constantly put your life into play, but you never made a true sacrifice." And though the son does not say this, clearly the father was not even a successful Nazi. But the object of writing the memoir was to be free of his father, to get him off his back, and that may be an impossible dream. This is a troubled family, and the sins of the grandfather seem to have been inflicted on the grandchildren. Sigfrid's daughter fell victim to extremist political ideas of both left and right, took to drugs, and committed suicide. Much of this troubled history features in his novel, *Winterhafen* (1999). All kinds of hidden pain remain.

Are the childhoods of these children of Nazi officials so intrinsically different from other childhoods? Every culture has its accounts of father-son relationships. In English there are those two Edwardian classics of Victorian childhoods, Edmund Gosse's *Father and Son* and Samuel Butler's *The Way of All Flesh;* a contemporary classic, Blake Morrison's *And When Did You Last See Your Father?* and in between, Kingsley Martin's *Father Figures,* to list but a few. Surely the young Gosse, brought up under the all-encompassing mindset of a Puritan evangelical father, had to endure every bit as much exposure to control as the young Sigfrid; and if Edmund Gosse responded in two divergent ways, assimilating this religiosity but also seeing an alternative set of cultural values in literature, his final showdown with his father might have been a better way for Sigfrid to free himself. There seems never to have been a real row, a clearing of the air, but instead a kind of sheepish attempt at keeping in touch. Still, there was a long period of apartness. Blake Morrison's memoir has curious analogies with Sigfrid's: both were written in response to a father's death, both had fathers who were doctors, Morrison's father was also right-wing and mildly anti-Semitic, both broke free from a father's influence and made alternative careers as teachers and writers. But Blake Morrison's wry, good-humored, and happy recollections of his father and of his childhood are a world away from the troubled searchings of Sigfrid, and maybe the burden of having a father like Herman with his appalling past was one that in the end radically impaired the son's chances of innocence and happiness.

ANTONY COPLEY
CANTERBURY, AUGUST 2001

## Notes

I should like to thank Ulf Schmidt for all his help in writing this preface, David Welch for pointing me in the direction of relevant literature, and also both the author and the translator for their help.

Gauch's first name appears as *Hermann* in official documents, and in *Vaterspuren* itself. But as an author, he spelled it *Herman,* believing this to be a more authentically German spelling; so *Herman* has been adopted here.

## Bibliography

Cecil, Robert. *The Myth of the Master Race: Alfred Rosenberg and Nazi Ideology.* London: 1972.

Frank, Niklas. *In the Shadow of the Reich.* New York: 1991.

Gosse, Edmund. *Father and Son.* London: 1907.

Mann, Erika. *School for Barbarians: Education under the Nazis.* London: 1939

Morrison, Blake. *And When Did You Last See Your Father?* London: 1993.

Padfield, Peter. *Himmler: Reichsführer-SS.* London: 1990.

Schneider, Michael. "Fathers and Sons, Retrospectively: The Damaged Relationship between Two Generations." *New German Critique* 31 (1984).

Sereny, Gitta. *The German Trauma: Experiences and Reflections, 1938–2000.* London: 2000.

# TRACES OF MY FATHER

# *1*

Turning off the alarm clock without getting out of bed. Then for the next few minutes, the usual morning ritual. Movements that make the wooden slats of the neighboring bed creak; the distinctive sound of bare feet on the carpeted floor (kitten scuttling in hot pursuit); the intermittent, not-yet-insistent wake-up calls from the living room; farther away, the coffee machine.

The telephone ringing unusually early, just before seven. From Marianne's heightened *Yes?* I can tell it is not my mother-in-law next door wanting to know her grandchildren's plans for the day. A soft, drawn-out *What?* from Marianne stabs me in my stomach.

I rush to the telephone—the word *Father* is on her lips—*Dead?* But I know already. I take the receiver. "I think Father has died," says Mother. "He is still quite warm, but he's stopped breathing." Growing impatience as she tells me more: that yesterday he went for a walk, said on returning he felt he had caught a cold; she was puzzled when he slept so late this morning when normally he was already looking at the clock when she came in from the next bedroom; that he didn't look as if near to death, for he lay sleeping, hadn't stretched out his hand to tap on the bedside table or switch on the light; hadn't called out either, for she would certainly have heard him through the open connecting door. "I'll come at once," I say, and "Please leave him as he is: I want to see him."

———

The scene I have so often rehearsed in my mind has come about. My reaction. Year after year, in autumn, fear and expectation that chronic emphysema, angina, arteriosclerosis, and diabetes would achieve their combined effect; that the Euphyllin injections that Mother gave him every night would no longer help. That the constant swings between near suffocation and breathing—implicit every night in the weather forecast after the television news—would be finally resolved.

Feelings spreading from my stomach all over my body.

The established routine: dressing, shaving, coffee, cigarette. Susanne, the eldest, is already at the breakfast table. "I've something to ask you, Daddy." "Not now, Susanne," I answer. "It won't take long," she says. "Your grandpa Herman has just died, I can't listen now. . . ." Shocked silence. Susanne hangs her head, sits stock-still; remains stock-still as I leave.

I should have called him up. I heard several days ago that he wanted me to call. Now it's too late. We saw each other for the last time four weeks ago, on the day I drove him to the village where he was born.

The ninety kilometers to my parents' house seem long. "Father," I say to myself, half aloud. I try to drive slowly, to keep all the speed limits. I imagine how it would be to be stopped by a police patrol for driving too fast. I would roll down the window, say, "Please let me off—my father's just died." I visualize the policeman's reaction on seeing in my face that I'm speaking the truth. I visualize his look of understanding.

The traffic is indeed held up: blue flashing lights of several emergency vehicles, a head-on collision in the early morning. One car lying on its roof, totally smashed, big pools of blood inside. I take in the details as I pass: the victims apparently already removed—it would have interested me to see them. "Drive by the book, now," I say to myself, and "Father, you are dead."

4

I recall the long solo car journeys when I would think about my father: the *Oberfeldarzt* (retired), the *Reichsamtsleiter* in the SS, the adjutant to Heinrich Himmler, the author of *New Foundations for Racial Research,* the man described by the chief prosecutor in the Eichmann trial as a "desk murderer," the man I knew: my father. I imagined how I would react to his death—I who by then at actual meetings with him exchanged hardly a fleeting handshake. I turn up the radio now, listen to the inanities of Südwestfunk's early morning show. I forget briefly why I don't have to teach at the school today.

A recipe given by the man on the radio takes on an unintended meaning: the marinade should be made first, then the veal heart should be cut up and placed in the marinade: "For two or three days the heart should lie still. . . ."

I arrive and park the car in front of my parents' house, where my brother and sister still live too. The door is opened the moment I ring: they have seen me come. My sister is in the yard bending over the baby carriage. She also must have taken a day off school. In the hall I see my mother and brother.

"Is he still there?" I ask. Their nods dispel my fear that he might already have been removed. I go to his bed. He is lying as always when ill: his head on one side, his right hand under his cheek, eyes closed, mouth slightly open. I sit on the edge of the bed, stroke his head, kiss him on the forehead, on his cheeks, stroke his shoulders, arms, and hands. I see my sister close to the bed, watching us, her child in her arms.

Washing my hands later I see in the mirror my own chalk-white face.

"I heard you were coming here yesterday"—his last letter to me—"to pick up the children, but it slipped from my mind, even though your mother said that she'd specially reminded me. That may be, but I didn't take it in. I've been quite confused recently:

last night I lay half dressed in bed till I realized I wouldn't have to fall in line. Yours, Father."

Confusion, similar to the dreams from which as a boy I would wake him in the middle of the night, when I would be woken by his groans and shouts and whimpers: for he was once again a soldier in the trenches, the seventeen-year-old volunteer who had taken his *Abitur* early in order to join up in the last weeks of the First World War, and had been so horribly wounded. He answered, when I asked him, that he'd dreamed that the French were after him again and wanted to shoot him: I'd called "Father, Father" hesitantly, then more and more clearly, until he woke up. I returned sadly to my bed, fell asleep, while he lay awake.

They were comrades together in the First World War, an old man from the next village told me later, at the burial. My father was just a lad when he volunteered for the army. To ensure acceptance at the call-up he had drunk, before he was weighed, two liters of water—else he'd have been two kilos short of the minimum weight of one hundred pounds. In the trenches my father had stayed close to the man for protection. He was scarcely more than a kid, repeated the old man.

He never killed anyone in that war—so my father told me a few months before his death. In the trenches at Soissons his duty was to direct artillery fire at targets picked out by his senior officer through a periscope. The officer announced that there was a French lookout post on the church tower of the village opposite and ordered him to fire. The first round of artillery had missed the tower by twenty meters to the left. Wanting to give the Frenchman a chance to leave his post alive, my father reported that the shells had landed twenty meters to the right. So the second round also missed. Confident now that the lookout had retreated to safety—if not, then it was his own fault—he fixed the range correctly. The third round destroyed the tower.

Lying in the trenches, he suddenly heard shouting behind him that sounded German—at any rate it wasn't French. In fact it came from the first deployment of Americans. It was terrifying to hear the rattle of caterpillar tracks: the first tanks, whose existence was not yet known. The frontal fire by the French was merely a diversion—the main attack came with the encirclement of the greatly depleted Germans by the Americans. Suddenly, shots from behind; the two men manning the machine gun were mowed down from the rear.

And sudden firing in Father's vicinity: splatterings of lead from the bouncing shells. One bullet pushed itself under his helmet, lodging in its thick lining. This is it, he thought, expecting to die, . . . but he had not died.

"I saw my hands, all covered with blood. The whole upper part of my body was covered with blood. The bullet must have ripped an artery in my temple. X rays still show splinters of lead in my skull. I pressed a bandage over my temple, but it went on bleeding. With both hands pressed on my skull, I walked to the first-aid post. I ran into some Frenchmen after barely twenty meters. No, no, I thought, I must go the other way! Then I saw some of our own soldiers approaching and I realized we were all prisoners.

"I was led away to the château at Rambouillon and lay there for three days and three nights on the bare ground. Several more bandages were applied to the wound, without effect. Then the wound must have scabbed over. A junior officer from Zweibrücken, who had also been imprisoned, shared his meat ration with me. Later he told me that he had thought my case was hopeless, that with such a wound no man could pull through. But he wanted to do at least something for me before I died. On the fourth night I dragged myself into the field kitchen and lay in the warm ashes of the fire. That saved me."

Sixty years, three months, and seventeen days later I see my father for the last time, see my chalk-white face in the mirror.

*1*

You were in reality a shirker—so it was said. In the trenches you knew only fear, pure fear. You clung to your old companions, never left their heels when distant shells were heard, when waves of explosions neared. You looked for father figures in the older soldiers, whimpered for dear life. You would, though, have condemned without mercy cowardice in others.

And your deeds of heroism were mere accident. Was the range you gave for the church tower an error, not deliberate at all? Did you make up the story out of shame, *Abiturient* that you were? In 1918 you wrote in a poem:

> *Calm—yet the enemy presses all round,*
> *out of trenches, in tanks, out of planes:*
> *and with all means of destruction he sends*
> *woe and death throes: trench-grave warfare.*

Yet you must have hated the enemy: hated and feared him. In another poem from this same year you wrote, "Sweetly the trusting warrior sleeps, knowing the guard his good friend keeps." No hero's words!

And in the Second World War, when right at the beginning you volunteered again, wasn't it mainly out of vanity? To gain promotion, so that you would be able to order a new uniform from the

best tailor in Berlin? You already had a whole closetful of uniforms—staff doctor (Marines), SA *Führer,* adjutant to an SS *Reichsführer,* district medical officer—and now you could add an
air-force officer's uniform! It was right and proper that the military drills you had taken part in over the years should bring you to
the next highest rank, wasn't it?

During the fighting in Yugoslavia you were mentioned in the war
report. You had lost your way and had picked up some soldiers
who had also lost contact with their unit. You took them under
your command. You marched on in the wrong direction till you
saw a town on the horizon ahead that you believed must be in
German hands, for you thought you were still behind the German
front. It was only when you stopped right in front of the town that
you realized that it had not been taken—that you were ahead of
the German front line. And weren't you afraid then? The towns-
people, thinking that you were the vanguard of more German
troops, hoisted white flags and gave up the town without a fight.
You declared yourself commander of the place, left some of your
men behind there, and proceeded onward. That was how, on 6
April 1941, you broke the main line of resistance at Marburg on
the Drau. For the capture of prisoners you received praise from
Flight General Löhr; for the taking of the enemy bunker you were
praised by Group Captain Baron von Weichs.

From there you continued to Samobar, this time accompanied
only by a driver and a soldier from the medical corps. Why? Probably because you were in very good spirits. What had worked out
once, from pure luck, without doing anything really, would work
out again, wouldn't it? And it *did* work again! You captured
Samobar—which was occupied by an enemy regiment—without
a fight. The regiment surrendered to you and your two soldiers.

And it happened a *third* time! Were you set on winning the war on
your own, with your driver and medical aide as your sole fighting
force, your jeep as your sole defense?

You reached the town of Agram. You were the first to get south of the Save—on 10 April 1941. In a standard work on the Second World War I find that "Occupation of Agram in Yugoslavia" is given as the heading for that day. You took Agram when the mayor walked up to you with a white flag, handed over the keys of the city, presented you with bread and salt.

You must have felt tremendously powerful then, and it was indeed quite a feat. Others would have asked for a whole division and—to be on the safe side—would have reduced the town to rubble and ash. Not you. There are still some photos stuck in your photo album. You are there, in the uniform of an air-force medical major, your jeep in the background, your driver next to you and a few inhabitants of the town. The medical aide took the photo with your Leica. On the back of the photo, in your handwriting: "From Raun to Samobar (occupied by an enemy regiment); advance to Agram south of the Save on 10.4.1941 (Iron Cross I); Serbian retreat to St. Marein observed on 11.4.1941."

Yes, you got an Iron Cross First Class for that. And you were mentioned in the war report under the heading "Notable Deed by a Medical Major." And in the standard works on the Second World War we find the "Occupation of Agram" by German military power. But not that *you* were that power, that you did it alone and it was pure luck.

In Samobar there was a regiment that gave itself up. A whole regiment! And it gave itself up to you and your two soldiers. You took—without a fight and without loss of blood—three towns that any other officer, eager for the Knight's Cross, would have laid waste. Did you perhaps save thereby the lives of hundreds of civilians and soldiers?

Later you received a letter from one of the two soldiers who were with you—who had meanwhile become an NCO. "Those hours," he wrote, "that I was honored to spend with you, during the six weeks that we served together, will always remain in my memory. Never before had I known the almost childish love for my commanding officer that I felt for you. When I took final leave of you in Graz, I was filled with a deep depression, which was actually justified, for from then on until the Russian campaign I was condemned to complete idleness, which was quite alien to my nature. Also in Russia I lacked a commanding officer from whom I could learn; so I had to fend for myself—and you were often in my thoughts."

In reality you were nothing but a shirker: somebody said that about you. I knew who it was who said it, but there was no need for you to know. The comment stuck in my mind. I was about eleven years old then. You never denied it, were not able to deny it, because you never knew of it. But you never invalidated it by telling me more about yourself.

That episode at Agram was but one of many that I learned about later and can prove. But why then those dreams from which I woke you because you were so terrified? In which you whimpered, moaned, called out "Help, help"? How did they fit in?

And then in April 1945, when the allies were already virtually at your front door, you declared yourself to be the area doctor for the Hitler Youth and tried to stop boys of fourteen or fifteen from fleeing the trenches they had dug against enemy tanks as forced members of the *Volkssturm*. You wanted to go against their parents, who were keeping their children at home, hiding them.

You truly believed that the war would be won with Hitler's "wonder weapon." Why did you want to hurl those terrified members of Hitler Youth into the front line, under the tanks? Was it because you had not pardoned yourself for your own fear in 1918? Yet you'd done all you could to save *enemy* lives at Samobar and

Agram. And you demoted one of your drivers because he had jauntily driven the jeep in which you were sitting over a verge on which a cat was sunning itself and killed it. You went purple with rage, yelled at him, tore off his air-force chevron.

You were said to be a shirker. I would gladly have asked you more questions. But I never did.

# 2

Papers stored in a bookcase, carefully ordered, labeled "In the event of my death." I look for what is required, notify the undertakers. On the way there I meet an old classmate. He's on his way to his office, carrying an attaché case. "No school today?" he asks affably. "No," I say. "My father has just died—that's why I'm free today." He laughs out loud, then apologizes, for it's not a laughing matter. His father died long ago.

I enter the undertakers' office and find myself in a storeroom with coffins piled on top of one other. While I wait, I pass my hand over the wood of the coffins: my father will lie in one of them today.

A middle-aged woman appears, greets me, offers her condolences when I say, "We've just spoken on the phone. My father is dead and needs to be buried."

She sits down at a desk in a side room, asks for the necessary particulars. Did his health insurance policy cover the cost of burial? When could the death certificate be collected? How many duplicate certificates did we need? Would we provide a suit or would he need a shroud? What sort of coffin would we prefer? It partly depended on the soil in the graveyard, whether oak or pine was better. How much did we wish to spend?

I decide—after seeing veneer coffins that looked like cardboard boxes—on a coffin made of oak, stained dark.

"He needs a pillow too," she says. "That will cost twenty-five marks. And fifty-five marks for a quilt." "He doesn't need a quilt," I say. "He won't freeze anymore." The coffin seller's face freezes.

And when could I supply the text of the death notice and in which regional editions of the newspaper should it appear? She puts a whole sample book of death notices in front of me, assumes (from the impression I have already given) that I favor a small-sized one. I can telephone later with the text. But I must first establish the exact time of the burial. If Father is to be buried in his birthplace, I must ring up the parish office: in villages the priest still fixes the time.

Which florist would we like for the flowers on top of the coffin, and did we want red carnations, chrysanthemums, or roses? Roses were dearest at this time of year; chrysanthemums cheapest. We would also surely need a basket of flowers to throw onto the coffin and a shovel to scatter some earth. Should the kind donations for flowers and wreaths be sent to the undertakers? And should the coffin be kept closed?

Mother sits at home by the telephone and tells relatives the news. "He died very peacefully, in his sleep," I hear her say. "He had a nice death." Her voice is quiet and calm. She is strong in situations that knock other people flat.

I ask her for warm water in a bowl and some hand towels. I begin to wash my father's corpse. I run a washcloth over his face and brow, just as I did sometimes when I found him very ill. His body is now ice cold.

I try hard not to have any feelings other than those I had when he was ill, when I shaved him, fed him, or gave him a bath. I lift up his head, pull his hand out from beneath it. No rigor mortis has yet set in. His fingers are as soft and flexible as before. But the hand that was under his head is discolored; there are red flecks on his body; his stomach is distended. I brush his teeth, try to close his jaw. But the tongue is too thick now, too unyielding.

While I wash my father, men from the undertakers' arrive. They have with them the coffin that I chose. Mother picks out a suit, freshly cleaned.

"No shoes," say the men. When they start to undress the corpse, we leave the room. "They wouldn't want to be watched by his relatives," says Mother.

My brother sits motionless in his bedroom, listening to music. I like that: I had myself switched on the radio, tuned it to some piano music, when I arrived at my parents' house. Someone had later switched it off. Mother is wearing black clothes now.

I enter Father's room again, when he has been dressed and laid out on the bed. The two men sprinkle chemicals onto the floor of the coffin before gripping him by the shoulders and feet to lift him in. They want to fold his hands together. "Please don't do that," I say. "That wouldn't be right for my father." The men look at me helplessly. They lay his hands on top of each other, but the hands won't stay there, they slip down to his sides. I myself try, without success. Then I bend over the coffin, kiss his forehead, stroke his hands. I move to the edge of the room, watch them putting the lid of the coffin in place.

I accompany the coffin out of the house. The hearse stands in front, with open doors and warning lights switched on. Laborers digging up the road interrupt their work and stare. I gaze at the departing hearse until it is out of sight.

A feeling of loneliness, welling up from my childhood; a mood of farewell, slight breathlessness, tears in my eyes.

"It was always a fault of his, never to say what he wished to say." So say the relatives in Einöllen, my father's birthplace, whom I look up this same day.

I tell them about our last visit to the church fete, when I drove Father there. I tell them how he rang me up because he wanted me to get a book for him in which there was an essay by him, a short autobiography. And he mentioned quite by the way that the Einöllen fete was due on the second Sunday of the month. "Would you like to go to it?" I asked him. "Not especially," he said hesitantly. "We'd have to drive there." "I'll gladly drive you there," I said, "if you'd like to go." He agreed eventually, but only after I had put it to him three more times.

My relatives nod knowingly as I tell them this. They understand well. For I often had to tease out his wishes in this way. He would say things quite by the way, but after many years of practice—sensing the undertones beneath what he said—I would push him to do what he actually deeply wanted but couldn't spell out.

Before Christmas or his birthday Father would always announce to the whole family that he didn't want any presents. He didn't need anything. Everyone still gave him something. But through that announcement he spared himself thanks, avoided having to show pleasure: he only needed to mutter that he hadn't actually wanted anything. Yet in fact he was often very pleased. I hear this for the first time at the funeral, from relatives living in Munich and Frankfurt, to whom he often spoke proudly of things that I thought had not been welcome to him.

Father visited me frequently at the boarding school in Meisenheim. I had to go there as a ten-year-old, for there was no other way I could attend a classical secondary school: a gymnasium. When I knew that he was coming I would run joyfully along the road from the classrooms to the dormitories. It didn't bother me at all that the prefect in charge of my lunch table sent me back to the washroom when I entered the dining room with hands not of the required shining cleanliness. Nor did it bother me to listen—sinking with hunger—to a prayer from the boarding-school chaplain or to be summoned by the housemaster's gong to take my place in the line for dishes to be shared out. I didn't need to force the food down that day—had no tears in my eyes if the teacher in charge made me eat up the pumpkin porridge that I usually found so revolting. It bothered me not one whit to have to poke around in the porridge till it was all finished, till the housemaster's gong announced that the meal was over and the second sitting could now take place. I had no trouble stuffing the whole serving of porridge into my cheeks, emptying the dish with the teacher standing nearby saying, "There you are—it isn't so bad after all," until I could run out into the open, spit it all out into the thickets along the recently built railway embankment.

For already I could see Father's car, stopping in the street.

We went together to the Town Hall Café, where he ordered a cup of coffee and a lemonade for me. He tested me on my vocabulary—Latin and Greek. Then he would lecture me on the relationship of particular words in German, English, French, or Slavonic, explaining that all these languages had a common Indo-European source and what the root of each word was.

I listened and nodded and forgot the boarding school.

Finally we read the magazines that were laid out there from beginning to end—though I read them from the end to the beginning, starting with the jokes on the back page. Father was chiefly interested in a series of articles in *Stern* about the daring flight and lucky escape of a German air-force hero from a British prisoner of war camp.

He told me about his own imprisonment in France after the First World War, in the citadel at Blaye in the Gironde: how, because of his reliability as a latrine cleaner, he received cigarettes and extra rations, which he then exchanged for bread. This he would slip to comrades who were ill, for whom the daily allowance of two bowls of warm soup was insufficient.

One of his comrades had to work at that time outside the camp and had noticed that the French guards—if it was too hot—hung their coats and caps on a nail close by the workplace. One day he took the hat and coat of a guard, went to the station, boarded a train, and arrived in Germany without any trouble. That had impressed my father and a friend greatly. They got hold of some civilian clothes, took the same way out, and were also undetected. On the train to Germany they consorted with dark-skinned colonial French soldiers, who wouldn't be so aware of their German accents.

When the *Stern* series was filmed with Hardy Krüger as the hero and Knight's Cross holder, I went with Father to a showing. He was very taken with the film. Around the time of his birthday, I saw in Meisenheim's single small bookshop the magazine series as a book. I had been saving my pocket money for weeks. I bought the volume for him, rejoiced at thinking of the pleasure it would give him, at having managed at last to find something that would interest him. He would no longer need to spend every evening he was at home walking up and down from the hearth to the window, from the window to the hearth. He would no longer need, each time he reached the hearth, to warm his warm fingers on the stove in that warm room and make that scraping noise when he rubbed his hands together. He could read the book, I thought.

"Here's a present for you," I said on his birthday and bowed my head. I felt my heart thump. He unwrapped the book, saw the title, and said, "I've already read that in *Stern*. Keep it for yourself—you can read it first." And he gave the book back.

That was the day on which I agonized for a full half hour about whether or not to plant a brief good-bye kiss on Father's cheek—and be tickled on the nose by his prickly stubble—as he sat in the car, motionless at the steering wheel, before I jumped out and up the steps into the boarding-school building.

The free time was over then. We sat at our desks and did homework. In each study room there were six desks; in every dormitory, six beds and six wardrobes. The prefect for each study room sat at one of the desks. He was a fourth-year pupil, a person with power and influence. The rest of us were first- and second-year pupils. If I did something displeasing to the prefect, he could pun-ish me—reduce my free time, for example, by confining me to the study room. Sometimes he tried to do that when Father wanted to visit me.

When Father had gone I would sit at my desk and pore over my schoolbooks. I would strain to read them, and the letters swam before my eyes. After a while I would say, "I must learn something by heart." I was then allowed to go into the dormitory for a quarter of an hour, where I would not disturb anyone by repeat-ing texts or vocabulary out loud. Talking in the study room was strictly forbidden—whispering too. The prefect clamped down on that severely.

Those minutes when I learned things by heart were the times that I most enjoyed. I often had things to learn—almost daily. I would stand at the window of the dormitory, gaze out at the roofs in the town, at the hills, at the families out walking with their children.

A sudden feeling of loneliness welling up; a mood of farewell, slight breathlessness, tears in my eyes.

After the drive through the Lautertal, past the villages, hills, and meadows that my father, sitting in the now empty passenger seat, had gazed at with eyes weakened by atrophy of the optical nerve, I park my car outside the house of his birth. I am recognized im-mediately, hailed with "Ah, Sigfrid—sincere condolences, we've just heard." I tell them what I've already told others: how he was here for the fete; how the journey had tired him; that he hadn't been well for years, you know, but that only yesterday he'd been out for a walk; that he hadn't woken up this morning; that he'd died a beautiful death.

"He lived his full span. . . ." The kindly meant, simple re-sponse.

The news of Father's death must have spread like wildfire through the village the moment that I made appointments over the phone with the priest and the burgomaster.

*II*

You meant it well—truly—when you rented a room for yourself in Meisenheim. I would not be so alone, and you wanted to keep an eye on my homework. You had given up your medical practice, and you had no other commitments.

At break, when the other children at the boarding school were free to play, I had to come to you. Either you waited at the entrance to the boarding school and we walked together to the Town Hall Café, or else I went straight to your room. There would be a bag with fruits of the season on the window shelf: in autumn, grapes—which I remember particularly because I loved them so much; in spring there were strawberries; in summer, cherries. I was always hungry because the food in the boarding school was never sufficient. While I ate the fruit, you tested me on my vocabulary. As I struggled to answer, the grapes, strawberries, or cherries seemed to stick in my throat. You knew all the words—you'd forgotten none—whereas I could never get them into my head.

The two free hours that I had in the afternoon would be spent in your room, grinding through "vocab." Then I had to race to get back to the boarding school in time for coffee with a piece of bread and jam—before "prep" began.

On the way into the dining hall I saw the others coming from all directions, in pairs or in groups, laughing and cheerful. I had come alone from your room, in which I'd been tested on vocabulary that I immediately forgot again. I found it quite fair that I should have to study while others played games. For when the others sat poring over their books, doing their prep, learning vocab themselves, I was free to slump and dream of freedom.

Joint study was completely taboo in the boarding school—even though the boy who sat dumbly at the opposite side of the table was in the same class as me. In the four big rooms on this floor about twenty-five boys studied. For the two hours of prep they were deathly still.

I shall never manage, I shall never learn, I thought, and dreamed of freedom.

You took great pains with me, kept a close eye—much more than other fathers. Before every test that we wrote in school, you stood at the school gate before school began or in the long break and asked for the most important words, crammed difficult Latin constructions into me yet again, lest I forgot anything. But during the test I sat with my mind as blank as a bare wooden board.

You even kept watch over my German, a subject that I enjoyed and got good marks for. If I had spent several hours writing an essay and was now allowed out into the yard, you would be standing there, waiting. While the others went to buy a snack, I had to come to you, tell you the subject of my essay. You would then give me a complete impromptu plan for the essay, with introduction and conclusion. Usually this was quite different from the way I wished to write it. You advised me not to express my own opinion but to repeat exactly what the teachers said. "One cannot say that today," you would say, "one must put it differently." You smirked and insisted on arguments that were the opposite of what you would normally, vehemently support. "If you write like this," you would say, "you will get a good mark." I was rather thrown by this and didn't know what I should think of you. In the early years I did you the favor of writing what you wanted. But later I stopped. Even when the newspapers were printing short articles by me, you still waited at the school gate with an essay plan up your sleeve. I only pretended then that your suggestions were a help to me. My actual essay was already finished, and in the rest of the lessons allotted for it I would write introductions, outlines, and conclusions for the classmates sitting all round me.

When the essay was returned to me with a good mark, I let you believe that it was the essay that you had formulated. You were happy and didn't read it through.

The other pupils played, while I learned vocabulary and immediately forgot it again. Others had friends and playmates; I had you, a father who watched over me. It wasn't until much later that I learned it was possible *not* to watch over one's sons like this. I thought of how you would react if I were dead, if I hanged myself and you saw my body. I shall never manage, I shall never learn, I thought.

I bent over my Latin vocab book and dreamed of freedom.

You truly put yourself out for me. One Thursday I went on a school hike with my class. On arriving back I met a school friend at the station who told us that our classroom had been broken into, tables and chairs smashed, maps torn, the whole room ransacked. When we reached the school—I was fourteen at the time—I went into the classroom building, curious to look at the mess. On the staircase up to our classroom I met our art teacher—whom we nicknamed Ox. "What are you doing here?" he asked, screwing up his beetling, bushy eyebrows and baring his teeth. "Looking at the classroom," I said. "I've heard that it's been smashed up." "Well, well," he said, "how have you heard? Who told you? You were all out on a trip today." "I heard on the way back, at the station," I said, feeling like a liar. "At the station, well, well," said the Ox, and his face lit up. "How interesting. How very, very remarkable." Then he bellowed: "You've no business whatsoever in the school today. Get out!"

I returned to the residence hall, terrified at having been

caught in the school at a time when I had indeed no business to be there. The Ox was hated, feared.

"Now I've got you all," he had shouted one morning triumphantly. It was the beginning of a new school year, and he was announcing to us that this year he didn't have us just for drawing but also for geography. From then on I got bottom marks for geography. The Ox, who had never studied it himself and had only been landed with the subject because of a teacher shortage, was always just one page ahead of us in the textbook. The grinds in the class noticed this and found it fun to ask—with an innocent manner and an apparent thirst for knowledge—about things they had learned two of three pages ahead in the book. He couldn't answer. But I never noticed that, for whenever I took the geography book in my hand, something within me froze. The letters swam before my eyes, and I put the book down again.

You would test me, at that time, on the rivers and capitals, imports and exports, and climates of the countries we'd studied. For each new country you'd buy me a box of Faber colored pencils. On each Faber box there was a map, and you'd scoured all the stationers' shops to find the right maps so that during oral tests and practice exams I could glance at the borders of countries and their capital cities.

So the Ox had caught me on the stairs. He came out of the art room with the smell of brandy on his breath—as always. During art classes (never in geography) he would disappear into his preparation room for a few minutes and return with the fresh smell of brandy on his breath.

He had put two and two together: I lived close by in the residence hall—as a bad pupil I was automatically suspect—so I must have been the perpetrator. He telephoned the hall immediately and I was hauled in for questioning. The housemaster confronted me with the charge: he sat in his office behind his desk, and I stood in front of it. Terrified, I denied it all.

I had to tell you about it then. You spoke with the teachers and the housemaster. The housemaster told you he was convinced that I was guilty, for on the stucco below the window—behind which I and the other boys slept—fresh footprints could be seen. So I must have scrambled out during the night. Although my room was on the upper floor, it would have been quite easy to use the ledge under the window to get to the downspout from the gutter. You listened to this silently. I didn't have to affirm to you even once that I was innocent: you believed me immediately. Why should I take this dangerous exit route when I could have used a window on the ground floor and—if I left it ajar—climbed in through it again? But the housemaster said that for him the most convincing proof had been that when he asked me about the ransacking of the classroom I had blushed.

You listened to this silently, as always. You nodded, then left. The next day you sought out the housemaster again in his office, told him that the residence hall's cashbox had been broken into and that the housemaster was the thief. "See how you are blushing!" he said in a voice that was trembling with triumph when the housemaster vigorously denied the charge. "Look at yourself in the mirror!" The housemaster saw his bright red face in the mirror. "When people are challenged to their face with crimes that they *have* done," you explained, "they turn white as chalk. When they *haven't* done it, they turn red. It's a simple biological fact. It's exactly what happened with my son."

The housemaster gave in to your argument. What you *didn't* know was that a few days previously the cashbox had indeed been broken into, and a pastoral assistant at the school had confessed to this. In proving my innocence you had intuitively chosen the right argument.

I was eternally grateful to you for this, felt deeply indebted. Suppose you had not trusted me? Yet I still had a guilty conscience. You never referred to the matter again. Could it be, I wondered, that you were *not* in fact quite convinced of my innocence and had only been so incensed for reasons of family honor? But I kept these fears—and my guilty conscience—to myself.

A little later I found out who actually had done it. I didn't tell you who for fear that you would have instantly reported it and exposed me to the boy's revenge. He was a boy from the same class, but older than the rest of us, because he'd been made to repeat a year twice. He was brutal—a thug. He had recently blown up a telephone booth with dynamite. He had ransacked the classroom out of lust for destruction. A little later he was expelled from the school for other offenses. As for the fresh footprints below the window, I knew how they got there the moment the housemaster mentioned them. But I didn't tell you that either—that the older boy who shared the room with me had come back late that night. Because the door of the residence was locked and our window often stayed open, he hauled himself up by the downspout, scrambled along the ledge to the window, and climbed into the room. He then crept along the corridor and down to the ground floor, and let his new girlfriend in through a window—a nurse whom he'd picked up that evening and brought back with him. "He's asleep," he whispered, when the girl saw me lying in the next bed. But I wasn't so fast asleep that I didn't hear the noises they made. I didn't fall soundly asleep till the girl had left the building in the dawn twilight, again through a ground floor window.

On the way to the classroom building I pictured in my mind a life in which there was no fear, no hunger, no discouraging teachers, no mistakes when my father tested me on vocab. A life in which there was no school after school, no coaching, no one emitting the same quiet groans as I'd heard from the Latin teacher in the morning.

On the way to the classroom building, before doing homework in math or Latin or Greek, or before a geography test from the Ox, I tried to calm myself with the notion that what I was now experiencing was not real; that I was not coming closer to the classroom, step by step; that I was not—in a quarter of an hour's time—going to sit helplessly in front of a duplicated sheet of untranslatable sentences; that in reality I was lying in a sunny meadow under a tree with my eyes closed and that all the rest was just a bad dream.

Or that if I could manage to walk on the paving stones without touching a line, maybe I would not be held back a year at Easter.

I'll get a five, I'll get a four, I'll get a five, I'll get a four: I would count my steps to the next turning like that.

For every third piece of work I did I would fall ill. Fever and a sore throat came as if by order. I shall never manage, I shall never learn—that's what I thought on my way to you.

I felt guilty because you meant well, truly well, when you rented a room in Meisenheim. I would not be so alone, and you could keep an eye on my schoolwork.

# 3

The village burgomaster works during the day for a firm in the town. He comes straight from work when I contact him.

"We'd like to bury my father here," I say, "where all his ancestors are already buried. We already have a grave in which my grandmother and great-grandmother are buried."

"That grave has been moved," he says, "to the opposite side of the cemetery, by the wall. The war memorial is where the grave lay before."

I gather that only the rim of the grave and the gravestone have been moved; the remains themselves have been left where they were. The claim to the grave would in any case have lapsed in four years' time. A new grave would have to be found, because the old gravestone too was no longer usable: it was as tall as a man, and the parish council's new regulations for the cemetery permitted no gravestone higher than eighty centimeters.

We agree on a site close by, in the old part of the cemetery. The burgomaster then calls the parish's handyman, asks him to inspect the site of the grave with me. It is already dark when we enter the cemetery. The man lights up the agreed site with a torch.

Four weeks earlier I had stood with my father here. On the way to the church fete we drove first to his mother's grave. It had already been moved to its new position by the opposite wall of the cemetery. Father supported himself with his right hand on a gravestone and his left hand on the handle of an umbrella, which he used instead of a stick. He was gasping for breath: despite the warm autumn day his emphysema was hard to endure. He said that without the Euphyllin injections that my mother had to give him several times a day, he would have died long ago. "You can be buried here," I said, "there's still room." He didn't answer.

The handyman told me that some years previously he had wanted to buy our house in Einöllen. It was old but still in good condition, although it had been empty for years. He would have converted the barn into a shop and renovated the house. Its position in the middle of the village would have been nice. But then the council bought it and had it demolished.

At present, the church fete's big merry-go-round stood on the site, and two or three stalls.

Meanwhile—he went on—he had got his job with the council. His decorating business was not going so well, so he worked at it for only three days a week, and three days for the council. That was a good arrangement: he would get a pension later, he had health insurance and job security.

We fix on the exact grave site. I'm happy with it. The handyman promises to prepare the cemetery morgue, organize candles. I press a banknote into his hand, take from him the address of the gravedigger, who lives in a neighboring village. On the way out he advises me to pay the gravedigger—an old man—in cash. "He needs the money," he says. "He often grumbles if his bill isn't paid within two or three days: says that he wouldn't have dug the grave if he'd known he'd have to wait so long."

In my jacket pocket, along with other documents needed for the burial—of no interest to anyone in Einöllen—I have a letter posted from Africa. It was written in the autumn of 1913 and reported the death of Father's father. My grandfather died when his son was just about to take the exam for entry to a gymnasium. Father had completed seven years at the *Volkschule*—the elementary school in Einöllen—and in addition had studied Latin, Greek, French, math, and history with the parish priest. When he arrived, in summer, to take the exam with other pupils at seven-thirty in the morning, he had already sat for two hours in the garden, reading Cicero or studying algebra from books lent to him by the priest. He should have been taken into the fifth year at the gymnasium, but by mistake he was tested on the curriculum for that year, which he waltzed through without difficulty. So the country boy with seven years of *Volkschule* behind him was placed in the sixth year, with classmates who were two years older than he was and had already done five years at the gymnasium.

"I haven't been able to get all the books yet," he wrote to his mother. If he couldn't get the rest (secondhand, he meant, or given to him for nothing), he would need some more money. But she needn't send him any for the time being: if necessary he would write to her again.

"Thanks to his conscientiousness, industry, and talent, he has succeeded to an extraordinary degree in overcoming the difficulties arising from the unusual course of his education." That was what Herr von Kennel, Headmaster of the Imperial Humanistic Gymnasium, wrote about him in his report of 14 July 1914. Herr Mülling, his form master, gave him a Good for his progress in German, Latin, Greek, French, math, and history; a Very Good in religion; and a Satisfactory in physical education—where he was up against boys who were one or two heads taller than he was.

My grandfather, who was a farmer and local councillor, belonged to the many from the Palatinate who supported their families by going to work abroad. He was often away for months in Britain, Scandinavia, America, or Africa. Then he would come home for a few weeks with the money he had earned and saved. The children were sired then too.

To finance his last trip, however, he used up his money—so

my father told me during our last visit to Einöllen. He had to borrow three thousand marks from a businessman in the village. With that money he bought some diamond mines in Africa. But he was cheated out of his entire investment by Jews in Amsterdam, who told him that the mines produced only worthless industrial diamonds. One day the businessman asked for his money back: all his parents' land had to be auctioned.

Otto, his eldest brother, who had pursued a career in the post office, became responsible for their mother and her three other sons. In the end, Grandfather got a job with the African Railway Company in East Africa. In his last letter he wrote, "Heaven has opened itself up to us now; the good God has helped us." He'd refused, however, despite the warnings of friends in South Africa, to have himself inoculated against malaria. He was an old African hand, he said: he wouldn't get malaria.

A few weeks later he died of it.


On the way to the presbytery I pass houses in which I played as a child. Lights are still on in the cowsheds. I have no feelings toward this village. Never in recent years have I had any desire to look at it again or to walk along the roads where I played as a child.

"A dead village," I say to myself.

# III

In recent years, when your attacks of breathlessness got worse and you could no longer sleep at night and were afraid that you were dying, you began to store up sleeping pills. You were a difficult, impossible patient. You gave orders all around, expected everyone to be at your beck and call twenty-four hours a day. "No one bothers about me," you said. "They find me disagreeable, claim that I'm not ill at all, that I'm putting it on." He wrote to me, "Ask your friend the lawyer whether I could sue them for slander. I'm living all day long amidst enemies, and that's the main cause of my distress. Please destroy this letter."

You threatened to kill yourself with pills. They had to be taken from you when you tried to carry out that threat, incensed at the suggestion that you should be taken to the hospital. Your colleague, who had treated you for years, recommended your urgent admission: it was high time. Your sphincter muscles were no longer working properly; some people said you were deliberately not allowing them to work properly. But I knew how quickly you might change again—become quite another person.

"The splinters in his brain are shifting," said your sister sometimes. "He's had them since the First World War; when he was X-rayed once, doctors mistook them for a tumor."

You yourself said that lack of oxygen was destroying your

brain cells: that was why you lost control of yourself during breathless attacks.

You remembered, no doubt, the evening when I was packing for my trip to London. The rest of the family had gone out for supper: a birthday was being celebrated, and you weren't well enough to go. Besides, no one had invited you. It was the first time in months that you were on your own again in the big house. There had been a row about it beforehand, and you had gone to pieces. "No one bothers about me," you said to me on the telephone. "They've all gone out. There's no sense in my living anymore; you won't see me again." And then, with voice cracking, "Farewell."

Panic stricken, I tried to get hold of relatives or acquaintances in the vicinity. After all, I lived nearly a hundred kilometers away. But I couldn't reach anyone. Then I dialed the emergency services, got through to the police in your area, told them what I feared you might do. I then dialed your number again, and you picked up the receiver at once. You told me tearfully that you had tried to hang yourself, but the rope had broken and the chairs had been knocked over and you were lying hurt on the floor near the telephone. "Someone will come at once," I shouted, "and I'll be there within three quarters of an hour. I'm setting off now!"

London, and the booking I had made for the journey there, were forgotten. As I drove to you I pictured what had happened. I shan't see you again alive, I said to myself—but in a corner of my brain was the thought, It won't be as bad as that this time, and then the counterthought, But what if that really is the case?

I didn't want to admit it to myself fully, but the hope was somewhere in me that I was free, finally, of the burdens of the last few years. I had several times offered to take you in with us, to look after you, even though I knew what problems that would bring; but you rejected the idea.

On arrival I saw a patrol car in front of the door. An officer opened the door for me, and I asked my first question in a whisper:

"Is he still alive?" The policeman nodded; his head and hand movement indicated that things were not too bad.

"Thank you for everything you've done," I said, and as he left I laid my hand on the leather arm of his uniform. "Thank you."

You seemed quite lively; your face had a self-satisfied look.

"I've cut my head," you said and showed me a place under your hair where there was actually nothing to see. "The doctor gave me an injection, and the policemen got me something to eat; I have to keep eating because of my diabetes."

You never asked me if it had been inconvenient for me to come. You knew that I had planned to go to London that night. You didn't try to make any excuse or apology. But I didn't expect you to.

At your request I rang up all the pubs in the town to track down the rest of the family. When I had no success, I went out to look for them myself. "Can I leave you alone while I go?" I asked. "Of course you can," you said.

I drove round the whole town, trying all the pubs. When I returned without finding anyone, I found the whole family there: they had just arrived.

Everything was in uproar. They didn't believe you had really been desperate. I understood well—though I didn't say as much—that your suicide attempt was symbolic, a cry for help. "You're mental," one of them said, "you should be locked up."

"You're an old scoundrel, a desk murderer with millions of Jews on your conscience," said someone. "You ought to be more apologetic. You knew exactly what you were up to, and if we'd known earlier how you would behave in this house, we'd have thrown you out. Moreover, after an event like this there'll automatically be an investigation of a suspected failure to assist in an emergency. You'll have to get us out of a right mess then! Don't imagine we'll lift a finger for you after this, you old scoundrel!"

"A nice spectacle you've made of us," someone said. "The whole neighborhood must be at their windows. All those emergency lights and sirens: ambulance, paramedics, police. You've landed us in the soup this time!"

I sat in the middle and said, "All this bellowing will get no one anywhere; it's pointless, it's no solution. You should try to discuss the situation calmly and change it."

"What is there to discuss and change?" said someone. "You've seen for yourself what a liability he is. Yet you always come running."

"You haven't yet cut yourself loose from him," said another. "At your age, it's high time that you did."

"You wanted him to be dead when you arrived," said someone who *had* cut himself loose from you. Or so he said.

"Where is the rope with which you're supposed to have wanted to hang yourself?" somebody asked you. "You've pointed at the pocket of your bathrobe, but even after repeated requests you haven't produced it."

"Look at the overturned chairs," you said. "Yes," said someone scornfully, "one can easily throw them about like that."

When the initial storm had blown over, I asked for a schnapps. On an empty stomach. It was a quadruple schnapps— but it relieved the tension.

Your illness was psychosomatic, you explained to me one day. You had consulted a psychiatrist, who had told you that. He said you lacked variety, contact with people. "It's not good for me to sit around alone in cafés all day," you said. "What can I do about it?"

I didn't answer by saying that you'd held yourself aloof all your life long, that you'd always sat in cafés, even as a young man, that you lived now as you'd always lived. To attribute your illness to that was a very flimsy explanation, if what was true now had also been true fifty years ago. It was your fault if you lacked variety; you pushed people away from you; you sat back and waited for people to make a fuss over you—just sat there, let all conversations hang in the air, hung your head, nodded, mostly said "Mmm." But I didn't say all that.

34

Nor did I say that you were never kind to anyone, that you'd accept kindness and help without saying thank you, without showing whether it pleased you at all.

Only in recent months had I heard for the first time, when I took leave of you, a thank you mumbled with your head bowed, or "Take care," or "Safe journey home."

I told you that your pension would be quite adequate, that you had saved long enough, that you should treat yourself a bit. "Go away somewhere," I said. You listened silently. You didn't react at all. I didn't know whether you had heard me, whether you wanted to hear me, whether you were waiting for another answer.

You yourself knew that the ostentatious store of sleeping tablets or the overturning of chairs was not the best way of starting to communicate.

The following noon I arrived in London, utterly exhausted. I sent you a postcard from there.

# 4

For the first time in twenty years I enter the yard of the parish office. Although almost all the houses in the village have been renovated or converted, the pastor's house is still the biggest and most handsome. It is the only one with three stories and a much bigger frontage than the one- or two-story farmers' houses that incorporate cowsheds and barns.

Whereas I remember the former pastor as a tall, noble, stern man, enthroned at his weighty desk or speaking earnestly and forcefully from the pulpit like a resurrected Luther, I meet his successor in the parish hall—converted from a barn—with children romping around.

I notice in the yard's lamplight that we are about the same age. He shows me into the official reception room, used for pastoral work or meetings.

I don't have to beat about the bush; I can talk openly with him. The pastor has obviously already established that my father had withdrawn from the church when he was a student and after the war had joined a free church—on paper, at least. "Yes, I know that," he said, "the German Christians, as they were called." During the afternoon the pastor has already heard various versions of Father's curriculum vitae—from his origins in the village to his role in the government of the Third Reich in Berlin.

"He was, it seems, Himmler's personal physician," says the pastor. He has no objections to burying him, but was that in fact right for my father? I am unprepared for this question: I assumed I would have to deal with objections on grounds of moral principle.

I falter, feel tongue tied: I say that the family has always been very religious, and through the centuries has produced sheriffs, pastors, lay judges, church elders; that Father's inner attitude had been stamped by that inheritance, that it had been suppressed by his thoughtless adoption—out of mistaken, humanistic idealism—of a false, criminal idea; that he had early on withdrawn from active politics but had clung to his ideals, had closed his eyes to reality, to evidence, right until the end.

As I reel off the explanations I have rehearsed earlier, I become even more unsure of myself.

"So would this Christian burial be right for him?" repeats the pastor.

I try to recall statements he made; I believe that he would surely have agreed with my arguments; I have in my ear the "Dead right!" with which a relative of mine in Einöllen had agreed with them too; that my father didn't think much of the church, but that I felt, nonetheless, he should be given a Christian burial in his home village. "Yes, I think he would have found that acceptable. I believe that honestly."

I recall snatches of a story that Father wrote in the 1920s; a few pages had survived the bonfire he had made of his manuscripts in May 1945. Before fleeing from the French, he had piled up most of his typescripts, offprints, and letters; poured gasoline over them; and set fire to them. He had turned the burning papers over and over with a pitchfork so as to leave nothing but ashes. Only the most important documents and papers had been wrapped in oilpaper and buried in a metal box.

——  ——  ——

"Free!" was the title of the "story of the coming rescue" that Father wrote on completing his medical studies, after which, according to the documents he kept, he had "impeccably demonstrated his solidarity with the campaigns in Oberschlesien in 1921 and Rhein-Ruhr in 1922 to 1923 as a member of the People's Brigades"—that is, as a member of the Ehrhardt Brigade—and then of the Sturmabteilung 520, whose commander was Rudolf Hess. In this story two elite troops clash during a battle for their homeland: the Red Guards and the Swastika Wearers. The leading figures in both companies—idealists and heroes—have traits that were obviously a self-portrait.

The ringleader of the Communists, Hans Rothart,

> was regarded as peculiar by his comrades. If they started to get raucously drunk, if they taunted their younger comrades with innuendos or direct barbs, or if the youngsters themselves joined in the debauchery, he would speak out against this and put a stop to it. They might well have wished to say that this was their only pleasure, that they had to enjoy themselves and no one should prevent it; but if Hans Rothart stopped it, they couldn't answer back. Of course he knew very well that this unruly social and sexual freedom was an essential cement that bonded them together and was even expected by the leadership; but he saw in it a numbing of the exalted purposes that should actually be theirs, and that was why he acted so firmly against it. He hated the irresponsibility with which his comrades and their girlfriends lived without regard for their descendants or their health, besmirching the natural decency of reproduction. And this hatred gave him strength and courage. It enabled him to be always first in the battle. He might easily have received some bloody wound by now, but again and again he came out unscathed and was always ready to volunteer to be first once again. For he sought death. His comrades knew that. And they obeyed him, even though he was not actually an officer.

Hans Rothart's opponent in the Hitler Sturmabteilung is called Erich Pope:

Slender as a willow wand, the company leader marched at the head of the column. He had taken his cap off his head and was carrying it in his hand. His white-blond hair shimmered in the sunshine. His head jutted out from his neck as if poised for attack. From the sharply chiseled features of his ruddy, neat, elongated face, his clear blue eyes looked dreamily into the distance. He breathed deeply. The decorations on his chest rose and fell. His gaze ranged over the company. What memories they brought back! The battles in Flanders, in Alsace, in the Tyrol, in Transylvania, in the Crimea, in the Caucasus, in Finland, in the Baltic, in Posen even after the cease-fire, in Upper Silesia, freeing German brothers everywhere! The decorations shone on his chest like the great history of his countrymen, like a promise of the future greatness of Germany.

— — —

The two companies—the Reds and the Browns—run into each other near Ratstedt: there is a shoot-out, and some men are killed. Then a horseman charges up at a roaring gallop, waving a white handkerchief. On hearing what sort of battle is going on, he turns his horse around and rides toward the other side.

Flares are ignited.

"They realized they should have stayed where they were. 'I think I know that man,' said one Red Guard to another as the horse charged through, despite being called upon to halt. 'Have you seen the bag with the red cross on it on his saddle? It's the doctor who was treating the wounded and the destitute.'"

A dialogue follows between the doctor and the company commander of the Reds:

"Damn it, comrades, what's going on here?" the horseman continued. "You're waging war in the middle of your native villages and are fighting your own countrymen—people who don't know you and have never done anything to you. Aren't you ashamed of yourselves?"

The company commander's answer came out pat:

"We're leading the people to freedom: that's why we're here."

"So you're fighting your own countrymen?"

"They are our enemies."

"Who are your enemies? Against whom do you actually want to fight?"

"Against capitalism!"

"And so you shoot people who are just as poor, are just as good workers as you are? Good grief! Go and meet your enemy first, and when you've come to know him then you can decide whether you want to fight him or not. Or are you perhaps afraid to approach him?"

"Afraid? No, quite the contrary!"

"Give the cease-fire signal!" shouted Wilhelm Heyd, the horseman, to an intermediary, and the company commander nodded in agreement. All stood amazed as they rode away together.

———

Brought together by Dr. Wilhelm Heyd, the enemy commanders meet each other, realize that they have long known each other, that at one time they were friends with the "same attitudes, the same nature, the same desires." The two companies—Communists and National Socialists—stand before each other: Wilhelm Heyd launches into a long speech of reconciliation.

He speaks with the phrases and rhetoric that were, at that time, not confined to the Hofbräuhaus in Munich. He talks of a conjunction of fate, of the symbolism of history—of world history, even: that here two companies, two ideologies were sitting opposite each other without fighting, who one hour earlier were deadly enemies. For whom were they fighting? For men behind them, whom they didn't themselves know. Patient, brave, bold, and honest as they were, they were willing to fight. But the man behind the Communists, that member of parliament Levy, where was he? And where was the castle-owning Baron von Waldstein, inciter of the Swastika Wearers? For that rich factory owner, Levy, that owner of many companies, the Communists were prepared to risk their necks—for him and his type, people who in reality wanted only to feather their own nests and, even more, wanted everything to continue going downhill so that they would have reason to rail against the misery for which they themselves were to blame.

"Don't you see? If things were to go well for you, they would be superfluous and would no longer have enormous, unearned incomes!"

But the National Socialists had been sent into battle by a landed nobleman who had not come along with them to defend his own land. Would they be rewarded for that, would he give away part of his immense property—which others had to farm for him because it was much too big?

"His workers have to farm the land and receive only a tiny fraction in return for the back-breaking labor they do to keep body and soul together—for slaving away for him all their lives long."

The basic cause of these injustices was a social order in which there were gentlemen and workers, in which people were not all equal: "people" meaning all German, all Nordic people.

On the last surviving page of this story the two companies—convinced by the words of the doctor—form a volunteer corps. In the Rhineland and the Ruhr they fight against the French occupation, against the "separatists."

I give the pastor a rough outline of my father's ideological stance, which—whether in this naive, never published text or in all his political statements and activities—won him hardly any friends, even in the Nazi government later. I tell him that my father was a dreamer who wanted the good but did the bad and the immoral. The pastor listens attentively, but keeps looking at his watch. He has left the youth group alone in the parish hall.

# *IV*

You never brought anything to fruition. Your whole life long you fought, but you never carried any battle through; you were not a fighter by nature. You never accepted a compromise, but you never pursued anything uncompromisingly to the end either. You repeatedly put your life into play but never made a real sacrifice.

No one—least of all myself—ever wanted this of you; I know that. But you always believed yourself to be a fighter, uncompromising and ready to sacrifice yourself. The demands that you made on yourself were—for yourself—never sufficient. Only you and your body noticed this: no one else. Your body responded with asthma, attacks of breathlessness, nightmares.

When I was doing badly at school yet again, you went to see the headmaster.

"If I become the education minister," you said, "I will make the teachers, not just the pupils, take examinations." And you also said, "As a former staff doctor in the army, I am equal in rank to you." You believed that you could influence him by this, hoped that he would instruct his teachers to give me better marks. You were convinced that after the next provincial election you would become education minister. You had joined the Deutsche Reichspartei (DRP), which had gained more that five percent of the votes in the last election and had one member in the state parliament. You were a member of the DRP's regional committee and headed its culture section. Fifteen years after the war you believed that the neo-Nazis could seize power.

You sent out briefing papers using the letterhead of the DRP's regional committee. In these you wrote of the witch hunts that the Catholic Church had launched against German citizens; you said that Catholicism had destroyed the German people. You compared the hounding of former National Socialists in the Federal Republic to the witch trials of the Middle Ages. You wrote about the extermination of the Jews, in which you tried to prove that the figures given for murdered Jews must all be lies; you calculated with your slide rule that given the size and number of gas chambers in the concentration camps (their total area in square meters), only a fraction of the official number of Jews could have been gassed, even if one assumed that they were piled into them body onto body and that the gas chambers were in operation day and night.

You wrote, too, about the crimes of the Allies. You wrote about Malmedy, about the prisoner of war camp in Bretzenheim near Bad Kreuznach, for example, in which thousands of German soldiers were killed.

You furnished, with your briefing papers, the chief grounds for the banning of the DRP.

The chairman in Rheinland-Pfalz of the Committee for the Defense of the Constitution wrote to you on this theme on 4 February 1960. His duties obliged him to write to you about several of your writings. His letter had no "Dear . . ." at the beginning and ended with the sentence "This closes all further correspondence between you and me."

This senior official had himself been persecuted by the Nazi government.

"The contents of the briefing papers of the Rheinland-Pfalz branch of your party, drawn up by you," he writes, "the material that contributed to the banning of the DRP, is so disgraceful and odious that I do not dare—in the interest of our country—to make it public. For, regrettably, these absurd concoctions do not merely reflect on their perpetrator and his party but will also be used and misused by evil-minded agitators against the Federal Republic.

"Do not believe," he goes on, "that it might not be known to me how, at the DRP's conference in Kaiserslautern, the party at the last minute distanced itself from you. When a journalist at the press conference on 9 January first raised questions about your writings, Herr Meinberg disowned them, and another party functionary described their contents—as did Herr von Thadden on the same day in Neustadt in front of the district administrative court—as idiotic. But I do not, in making this point, wish to adopt the opinion of these gentlemen in case I provide you with a legal handle against possible criminal proceedings under our constitution.

"I do not yet reliably know," he goes on, "whether you—who have made no secret, in your briefing papers, of your hatred for the constitutional order of the Federal Republic—are drawing a pension from the federal or state government. You should seriously consider whether it is appropriate to allow yourself to be looked after by a state whose destruction you seek."

You preserved this letter, and I came across it again in a collection that you labeled "Intellectual Visitors Book," a kind of scrapbook of letters from personalities you admired and believed in. The letter lay among them as a curiosity; next to the name of the author of the letter you had written in pencil in brackets the word *Jew*.

In this "Intellectual Visitors Book" there is a series of personal letters to you. The senders of the letters read like a history of a bygone age. They include:

> RUDOLF HESS, DEPUTY FÜHRER ("I thank you warmly for the kind dedication. Heil Hitler!" The Deputy to the Führer, 30.11.34).

HEINRICH HIMMLER, REICHSFÜHRER SS AND INTE-
RIOR MINISTER ("The 34 reichsmark have been paid.
I have also authorized a further 1000 reichsmark for
the rounding off of the plot of land. . . . Heil Hitler!"
The Reichsführer SS, 13.7.34).

OSWALD POHL, OBERGRUPPENFÜHRER SS AND GEN-
ERAL OF THE WAFFEN-SS ("I was very sorry that we
missed each other in Munich. I should be delighted if
on some future convenient occasion you could visit
Munich." With best greetings. SS Administrative
Headquarters, 9.5.38).

KARL WOLFF, GENERAL OF THE WAFFEN-SS ("Unter-
sturmführer Dr. Herman Gauch, Adjutant to the Re-
ichsfuhrer SS, has permission from his Command to
be away in Saarland from 1 to 4.3.35." SS-Ober-
führer and Chief Adjutant to the Reichsführer SS,
28.2.35).

MARTIN BORMANN, PARTY MINISTER ("Herr Hitler
asks me to thank you warmly for your suggestions.
With German greetings." Office of Adolf Hitler. p.p.
Bormann, 10.3.32).

JULIUS STREICHER, GAULEITER OF FRANCONIA ("We
thank you for your energetic assistance and very
much hope to hear from you from time to time. Heil
Hitler!" From the *Stürmer,* Editorial Department,
4.11.36).

RICHARD WALTHER DARRÉ, FARMERS' LEADER AND
MINISTER FOR FOOD ("If I ask you to write these
essays without giving your opinion of Christianity, I
am influenced by purely political considerations, not
my own point of view. . . . With German greetings,
Yours." Minister for Food and Agriculture, 8.7.33).

WILHELM VON SCHOLZ, WRITER ("Thank you for

your good wishes, love and friendship. . . . Very sincerely." Dr. Dr. v. Scholz, 15.7.64).

KONSTANTIN HIERL, REICH LABOR SERVICE LEADER.

JÜRGEN SPANUTH, RESEARCHER ON ATLANTIS.

OTTO CARIUS, HOLDER OF THE OAK GARLAND, THE KNIGHT'S CROSS, AND THE IRON CROSS, AUTHOR OF "TIGER IN THE MUD" ("For there were also in the early years so many incompetents in the Army, who have now had to be brought back into the ranks; and I am pleased to tell you from my own experience that the younger officers are sound, while the many unsuitable older men—whose sole qualification was often that under certain circumstances they could recognize a 'resistance fighter'—are gradually being pushed to the sidelines. . . . With best greetings." Carius, Hirsch Pharmacy, 29.1.61).

LUDENDORFF, COMMANDER IN THE FIRST WORLD WAR ("My thanks and greetings!"April 1924).

GEORG WILHELM, PRINCE OF HANNOVER, BROTHER OF QUEEN FREDERIKA OF GREECE ("It interests me greatly to read about your researches, that are in part quite new to me . . .").

THE HEADMASTER OF THE CASTLE SCHOOL, SALEM, 13.9.56.

ROBERT SERVATIUS, DEFENDANT IN THE EICHMANN TRIAL ("I would be very grateful to you if you could send me two photocopies. The number of actual victims is of significance not only for the extent of the blame but also for the demand that injustice be made good. Respectfully." 29.7.60).

ADOLF HEUSINGER, INSPECTOR GENERAL, ARMED FORCES.

Kurt von Schleicher, Reich Chancellor.

Wilhelm Groener, Defense Minister.

Professor Dr. Friedrich Karl Günther, anthropologist ("But I am delighted that, from various sides, questions of belief formation are no longer being aired. . . . Closest greetings from one who is wholly devoted to you." 12.9.34).

Friedrich Wilhelm Brückner, Hitler's Adjutant, Commander of my regiment, 1922 ("It will be handed to the Führer at a suitable opportunity. . . . With German greetings." Head of the Führer's personal adjutant's office, 13.2.40).

Fritz Schneider, Justice Minister in Rheinland-Pflaz ("I believe much more that it is my duty to make known to the public the dangers that lie in the laws that have been announced by the Federal Government. . . . With highest esteem." 12.1.67).

Hans-Ulrich Rudel, holder of the highest German medal for bravery ("I would be delighted to have the chance to hear from you again. Best wishes and greetings to you and your comrades, Yours." 24.6.59).

Dr. Arthur Gütt, in charge of the rules for the prevention of hereditary diseases ("We need a reorganization of the public health service. The formation of offices, race offices, etc., should not happen till then, for a forthcoming law will regulate all these questions. . . . With German greetings and Heil Hitler!" Interior Ministry of the Reich, 7.8.33).

Paul Ratz, defense lawyer for Alfred Rosenberg, my schoolmate.

PROFESSOR DR. JOHANN VON LEERS, FOLKLORE RE-
SEARCHER. ("I know Colonel Rudel from my time in
Argentina—he visited me in Cairo just a few weeks
ago. . . . We should totally reject and not use anymore the stupid, brainless word "anti-Semitism,"
which only the Jews have introduced in order to
hide themselves behind a decent racial family that
only they did damage to. I am for the Semites because I am against the Jews. I revere, for example,
the great Semitic king Salmanassar of Assyria, who
impaled hundreds of Jew-devils all over conquered
Samaria. . . . We who are enemies of the Jews and
their tradition and tyranny find true allies in speak-
ers of Semitic languages, especially the noble Arab
race. I enclose a valuable memorandum with the request that you will disseminate its contents. . . .
With heartfelt good wishes, your old and true ally."
Méadi, Cairo, 5.6.1959).

HEINRICH HELLWEGE, PRIME MINISTER OF LOWER
SAXONY ("Your reference to the inadequate application of the code of occupation in the French zone seems
to be correct from my own observation, as a few days
ago an officer of the French gendarmerie clapped a
fine of DM 10 on me because my car had a minor
lighting fault. In your case the infringement of the code
was obviously much more serious. . . . With highest
esteem." Minister for Parliamentary Affairs, 9.11.49).

WILL VESPER, WRITER.

KURT SCHMALZ, GAULEITER OF HANNOVER.

KARL DÖNITZ, HIGH ADMIRAL AND REICH PRESI-
DENT ("You correctly allude to my position under
international law. The present business is, however,
legally and materially without any foundation, and

will be settled without recourse to international legal considerations. Sincerely yours." High Admiral, Retired, 26.9.65).

PAUL VON LETTOW-VORBECK, INFANTRY GENERAL AND LEADER OF THE PEACEKEEPING FORCE IN GERMAN EAST AFRICA.

PROFESSOR DR. WILHELM HAUER, LEADER OF THE GERMAN FAITH MOVEMENT.

ADOLF VON THADDEN, WRITER, LEADER OF THE DEUTSCHE REICHSPARTEI.

GREGOR SCHWARTZ-BOSTUNISCH, HEAD OF THE FREEMASONS' AND JEWS' ARCHIVE IN BERLIN, ADMINISTERED BY ADOLF EICHMANN ("I'm afraid that since 1936 I have had nothing more to do with the Archive; in 1937, at my request, I was made Obersturmbannführer in the 6th Unit of the SS. My career is now at an end. From 31.8. till 5.10, as I lay in the Munich Surgical Clinic, suspended between life and death (operated on twice), only the Reichsführer SS thought touchingly about me. Nobody else. I'm very pleased to hear from you again before I die. . . . Heil Hitler! Yours." 8.11.42).

ADOLF HITLER, FÜHRER AND CHANCELLOR OF THE GREATER GERMAN REICH (Sturmabteilung 520. On behalf of the Works Committee: Adolf Hitler, 3.11.1922).

FRANZ JOSEPH STRAUSS, FEDERAL DEFENSE MINISTER ("You confirm me in the view that, concerning the great questions of state security, one has to decide between duty and convenience and also take account of the disadvantages arising therefrom. All these things can be judged only in a broad perspective.

Yours faithfully." Dr. honoris causa, Federal Minister, 14.12.62).

Hermann Ehrhardt, Leader of the Ehrhardt Voluntary Brigade ("I think with pleasure and without regret about the past time of conflict and I'm delighted when I hear that an old fighter is still well. I've written a few lines to the editor of *Kristall* under the motto 'What does it matter to the moon if a dog barks at it?' . . . With comradely greetings." 16.1.63).

Otto Skorzeny, Liberator of Mussolini ("These new slander campaigns against me have not in fact surprised me, for my friends—whom thank God I have all over the place—told me about them in good time. . . . Yours faithfully, and with best thanks in advance." Madrid, 8.3.63).

————

The letters are arranged in that order, and there are a whole lot of names still to mention: names above all of "race researchers" whose books led the way to genocide and accompanied it and who after 1945 still retained their professorships, and names of writers whose work continued to be published by respectable publishers after 1945.

Himmler's letter to you shows how he consciously controlled every reichsmark that you spent on erecting the memorial in Verden-on-the-Aller to the "Baptism-Resistant Germans Massacred by Karl, the Slaughterer of the Saxons." Through him you got to know Johann von Leers, Party Orator from 1929 and from 1938 professor in Jena of German history with special reference to peasant history, who in 1945 fled via Argentina to Egypt, converted to Islam and took the name of Omar Amin von Leers. He had a leading position in the Propaganda Ministry there, and often instructed one of his staff—a Mr. Sadat—to send you packets of anti-Semitic propaganda material.

You never brought anything to fruition. After you gained your doctorate you wanted to pursue an academic career. Darré, the Minister for Food, recommended you for a professorship, but nothing came of it—because the Finance Minister abolished the post, so you said. You gave up your career as a navy doctor after only a brief period as the director of a navy institute for hygiene and bacteriology—because the navy laid a charge of high treason against you for your propaganda activities for the Nazis, so you said.

As Himmler's adjutant you were, you asserted, in the position of a general, with considerable powers; there, as in the Agriculture Ministry, you converted advisory papers into laws, some of which are still valid today; but after a year you were decommissioned—because of lack of expertise and friction between higher staff members, according to what you wrote in your military CV.

Your post as a district doctor lasted only half a year—because Gauleiter Saarpfalz did not renew your contract on grounds of political unreliability, so you said.

As a state-employed doctor you worked for only a few months; as a doctor for patients with medical insurance, you practiced for only a few years: they took away your license because of your party activities, so you said.

As a senior staff doctor, you dropped out in the middle of the war—because you thought the war was already won, so you said.

After the war you applied for a practice, but you didn't get one. You took on work as a locum, but when you were invited for a second time, you declined on health grounds.

You wanted to be Culture Minister for the DRP, but you left the party shortly before it was banned.

You joined the march to high military rank too late. The blood orders that you set such store by were never awarded to you.

You wrote in an application letter to the Federal Minister for Defense, "I was in the political sense active only in military organizations, never as a political leader." The army was being rebuilt, and you would gladly have been a medical general in it. You were rejected—because you were too old, so you said.

On 3 January 1949 you were classified by the main Denazification Committee for Stade District as belonging "to the discharged group (Category V)." The cost of the proceedings was fixed at DM 20. As treasurer of a local Nazi group, you would not have dared dream of such a decision. It was based on the following:

> The accused was a member of the NSDAP from 1934, but without office.

Correct, because during your service with the navy you had to keep officially quiet about your party membership.

> The accused belonged to the National Socialist Welfare Organization from 1936 till 1944 and to the National Socialist Doctors' League from 1934 till 1944, but without office. The accused was also for a while active as a doctor in the Reich Labor Service.
>
> These statements are based on the submissions of the accused himself.
>
> No other burden of guilt on the accused has come to light.
>
> According to witnesses, the accused was not prominent with regard to National Socialism. The accused is discharged, as he belonged to the NSDAP merely in name, did not influence it, and—apart from the required membership fees—did not give it financial support. This decision is based on Paragraph 7 of the Legal Ordinance of 3.7.1948. The decision on costs is in accordance with Paragraph 3 of the Fee-remission of 26.4.1948.
>
> Evidence: submissions by the accused. References:

And names follow of old army comrades who had actively supported you back in the 1920s and for whom you on your part supplied testimonials that they had not actively supported the Third Reich.

———

You said once, with a smirk, that you had not lied. In the famous denazification questionnaire you had written in large capital letters and had begun with the harmless organizations, such as the National Socialist Doctors' League. The lines were then full, and you were able to leave out the rest with a clear conscience: you would, if asked, have been able to explain that you couldn't fit any more on the lines.

When the discharge was enacted, you were able to forget your fears about the report you had sent to Reich Security Office in the last days of the war, when the Americans were advancing on the village: a report in which you described things being said by prominent villagers that were sapping morale. "If that had fallen into the hands of the Americans," you said, "they would have hanged me."

As an SS Oberführer you were assigned under a false name to the SD—the Security Service.

When the discharge was enacted, you could boast about how you went underground in 1946.

When the Americans arrived you were not charged with anything. The French too had handled you favorably as a doctor—differently from the rest of the population, you said.

In April 1946, Ludwig Moses, a Jew who had taken over the denazification hearings in Kusel, summoned you there. He said that he knew you as a Swastika Wearer back in the 1920s, when he was a cattle dealer in Einöllen. At the end of the deliberation he wanted to telephone the French to ask them to arrest you; but it was twelve noon, and the French had gone for their lunch.

You used this moment to disappear in your car, to Rockenhausen. You got permission there from the French authorities to help your sister-in-law move her furniture "from Dörrmoschel": there was a Gauch family living there, should questions have come back to you. The authorization was issued without any further enquiry, because the French were happy to let those who were not from the Palatinate move away—and your sister-in-law was from Worpswede.

That was how you managed to get her away with her children, and your sister too, and all your and her furniture in a moving van. But you yourself drove me and Mother to Worpswede. The journey took three days because of several punctures. In Unkel you simply went to a doctor, who guided you along field paths and through gardens over the border between the French and British occupation zones.

At Osnabrück you reached a British checkpoint. Your car had a white-and-red ring as a badge, signifying permission to drive at night in the French zone. But because in this area there were many Poles working for the British, the badge was taken to be a Polish emblem, and we were allowed to drive through.

The German authorities—and also the French (because of the denunciation they had issued against you) had sent out a search order by then and would have had you arrested if they had known where you were.

You managed to go underground. You applied to the English for a military function, for you knew that in that case no one would hand you over.

In Verden-on-the-Aller you were made a troop doctor with waffen-SS units that were quartered by the British and were still, in part, armed. You got British military papers from the navy headquarters in Minden and Hamburg. To be on the safe side, you even turned up at the naval office in Wilhelmshaven and were received there.

Later, for understandable reasons, the fact was covered up that the British, for fear that the Russians might plan an incursion over the occupation border, deployed armed SS troops in a deliberate raid against the Russians. They retained complete administrative autonomy and lived as if they had not lost the war.

As a British military doctor you then used military train tickets to travel all over Germany.

"Such oddities," you said, "gave privileges to underground fugitives like us."

You preserved your identification papers.

You certainly fought your whole life long. But you never carried any of your battles right through. You were not a fighter by nature. You made no compromise, but never laid yourself on the line. You constantly put your life into play, but never made a true sacrifice.

# 5

On waking up, my first thought is that I shall never see Father again. That his body last night has decayed a bit more in its screwed-down coffin in the cold morgue. That I came home late in the evening with a marvelous sense of calm; that I slept deeply and soundly.

I remember that I dreamed about Father: that he stood tall before me, came down a staircase or was in a house; that he said something; that I seemed to face him as a young boy, for I had to look up at him.

I remember that in the dawn twilight, half asleep, I still had this dream clear in my mind; that I wanted to write it down, but was not properly awake.

I get ready for school.

Everyone in the staff room behaves as usual; I too. We talk about trivialities, laugh. When I come to mention what has happened, I do so unemotionally—in the way that one speaks of the death of a stranger. But I say that his death—even though it was only to be expected at his age—has wounded me.

The children in my class react sweetly. The reason for my absence the previous day has been explained to them by the substitute teacher. "Please wait a moment," they say, "there's something we must do." They huddle over a bench and write. Then the form captain hands me an envelope with a black border.

They sit still and watch as I open the envelope and take out the card on which "Sincere condolences" has been printed and which all the pupils have signed.

They must have decided on this yesterday, must have detailed someone from the class to buy a card. They take pride, clearly, in pleasing me with it.

They are children with learning difficulties: truants, dyslexics, children from marginal groups, from socially deprived backgrounds, children with slight mental disabilities. Some of them have lost their fathers; one was present when his father poured gasoline over himself and set himself on fire; many of them don't know their fathers; a boy must decide in a court of law in two days' time whether he wants to live with his father or his mother; a girl is living with her eighty-year-old grandmother and is fearful of the day when her grandmother will die and she will have to go into a home.

They are children who are full of sympathy and compassion if someone they like appears to be suffering, full of aggression if anyone rejects them. I tell them about the death of my father, of how he had to suffer for many years, how he passed away calmly.

In the classroom today there is a different mood—hard to define: the same sympathy but more reflectiveness, more dreaminess.

In Einöllen today I have to make the arrangements for the burial. The cemetery lies outside the village on a hill, surrounded by fenced-in pastureland that is still—this late in the year—grazed by cattle. It's a sunny, cold day.

The gravedigger has already started his work: an old, bent man with arthritic, work-worn hands. He is hacking at the stony ground with a pickaxe and shovel.

I photograph him as he gouges out the hole for my father. He asks for a copy of the photo; I promise to give him one. He poses himself in the grave, holds the shovel like a weapon when standing at ease, remains motionless until I have pressed the shutter.

He tells me how Father once saved his life: How his own family doctor had prescribed a simple household remedy when he described on the phone his agonizing symptoms and had told him to come to the office the next day. How when he was at the end of his tether his wife had gone to my father, who by then—because of his own ill health—was no longer practicing. How Father had immediately come over, had arranged admittance to hospital, and had thus forestalled an imminent burst appendix.

For about twenty-five years—until the church fete four weeks ago—I had visited no one in the village. I now remember a friend of my aunt—a distant relative—and I drive to see her, to ask for her help and advice.

I learn from her about everything that has to be done for the gathering after the burial, the coffee and cakes that have to be organized: who to order the cakes from—preferably ring cakes and crumble cakes, half of them from the "upper" baker in the upper part of the village, half from the "lower" baker in the lower part—that is what one does here. Coffee, milk, and sugar should be bought from the Woll sisters, the two octogenarians who run the only grocery store in the village. I will also have to hire the parish hall, and women would be needed to help with the refreshments.

I tell her that I don't know anyone anymore; also that I don't know who in the village is closely enough related to be invited to the gathering.

Aunt Anna's friend, whose daughter is the village postmistress and has daily contact with all three hundred inhabitants, helps me draw up a list.

Can I, I ask her as I deliver the invitations, ask those who are relatives to help? Of course, she replies: it will be an honor—no one will say no.

The first visit I make is to a female cousin of my father's, the same age as he, who herself is close to death. During the church fete Father sought her out; they sat down next to each other, ate cakes, spoke of old times, were photographed by me—the last photos that show them both alive. Klärchen (the cousin) was full of grumbles: she was in a bad way and even had to give up her shop a few weeks back—just imagine! What on earth was the matter? "Herman," she asked him repeatedly, "will I get better?"

Father wrote her a prescription: something that I myself take and which has often helped me.

Aunt Klärchen, as everyone in the village calls her, never got married, and for sixty years ran a shop with the sign "General Store." She was always at hand. If one noticed at noon on Sunday that there were no eggs left in the house, one knocked on the back door behind her house. If at nine o'clock in the evening one ran out of tobacco, one could call her up. If one needed to telephone urgently, one could use her phone. And if an important telephone call came to Einöllen at night, it was taken by her, and she would immediately march around to inform the required person.

She always had a few sweets on her. As children we made full use of this. My friend Willi and I once sent my sister—three years old at the time—into the shop with a few pebbles in her hand to buy some sweets. Aunt Klärchen, seeing through everything ("Those naughty boys have sent you, have they?"), was touched nonetheless and gave Gudrun the desired handful. We took the sweets from her outside the shop: she got just one for herself, as a tip.

Aunt Klärchen's sister from town is there to nurse her. No point in taking her to hospital, the doctor has said. She's nearing the end: she just needs someone to sit with her and watch her.

She is already in a coma when I reach her bedside. She no longer has her false teeth in, so her nose and chin stand out sharply. Her mouth is just a small round opening. She's wearing a frilly nightdress and is breathing heavily; with one hand, she keeps trying to pull off the bedclothes, then draws them up to her neck again. Then she suddenly becomes calmer. She lies still; her breath slows down, can suddenly be heard no more. Her chest no longer rises and falls. We wait expectantly.

"It won't be long now," whispers Klärchen's sister to me; but then her breathing slowly starts up again.

"It's been like this for three days," her sister says. "She hasn't eaten anything for a week, and from yesterday has taken no fluids either."

I stay a while longer beside her bed; the stertorous breathing sets in again, the restlessness. I stroke her hand in farewell. I wonder at my own inner calm.

The Wolls' shop, with the sign "Woll Sisters: Groceries," is just behind the place where our house once stood. The bellpull is exactly as it was in the days when the two sisters already seemed immensely old to me. I stand in the gloomy entrance hall and try to reawaken the feelings I had before, when the shop seemed mysterious and desirable: no display window, just a small side room in a former farmhouse, shelves on each wall, stuffed full of goods of all kinds, from sewing thread to Four Leaf Clover milk; only space for two or three people in front of the counter. If there are more—which is seldom the case—they must wait in the hall.

Blondie, the younger of the two, enters the dark hall. I introduce myself and am led—amidst the cries of surprise that follow her expressions of condolence—not into the shop but into the living room. Next to a coal stove, which emits a fierce heat, sits Hilda, the elder sister, with a woolly blanket over her knees. I recount once again my father's death.

"How nice," they say, "that he is coming back to Einöllen. We can't, alas, go to the burial, for the suppliers all come in the afternoon, and we shall have so much to do. But we shall send a wreath, of course."

60

They accompany me into the shop and advise me on the quality and quantity of coffee, which I note down.

"Kaffee Hag is what is mostly drunk here: take that, Sigfrid," they say, "and sugar of course, yes, yes."

"Milk too, Blondie, give him some milk. There, that's the milk—no, not that, pass me the other, Blondie, that's the one, it's better."

"Yes, yes, Hilda, you're right, it's better," says Blondie.

"That will be enough," they say, but I want to take a bit extra. I tell them, "I can take home what's left over."

"Yes, yes, you're right: one always needs it."

They stoop over a small piece of cardboard that they have cut to the exact size of a cash memo and work out the bill.

They tell me I can leave the things there: they'll be delivered on time to the parish hall. And I'll get a proper receipt then too, of course.

I remember how as a child I got the same cardboard cash memos from them, cut from grocery boxes.

While Blondie adds up, Hilda looks for her glasses, then checks the column of figures, discovers a mistake, and, with soft cluckings of disapproval, corrects the final sum. Even this is a scene I clearly remember from before.


I used to dislike shopping. Perhaps my fear of shops stemmed from an accident that is deeply engraved in my memory.

Opposite the "small school"—a room in which years one through four were taught by Herr Schmidt—there was a shop that was the only one in the village that also sold toys. After school one day I was impelled to draw something on a tree in front of this shop—with a stub of chalk I had found. The shopkeeper—the son of the man who had put my grandparents' plot of land up for compulsory auction—came rushing out, roaring and cursing, and chased me off. I ran away, frightened to death, but looked back to see the man, in his white coveralls, stumble and fall headlong into the filth of the street—the sewage that flowed along the gutter. There was no main water supply or drainage in the village: just wells for drinking water and cesspits.

Thereafter I gave the shop a wide berth and went home after school by a different route—always fearful that the shopkeeper would come storming out again to deliver the blows that had been prevented last time.

When at New Year my father wanted to buy me a cap pistol there, I stayed outside with my heart thumping. Father called me to come in. "He should stay outside," said the shopkeeper when he saw me. Father simply looked at me, raising his eyebrows and adopting a typical expression, half ironic, half ashamed, and said nothing. On the way back he said nothing about the incident.

I pictured to myself how it would have been if Father had instead retorted indignantly, "Well! If my son may not enter this shop, you won't see me again here either!" How he could have slammed the door behind him and said to me, "That will teach him!"

For many days afterward, firing the pistol gave me no pleasure at all.

I liked drawing.

I thought of how my teacher at the time had said on the telephone that I might be an artist one day.

After my first school report, at the beginning of the holidays, I suddenly saw him standing behind the counter in the baker's shop—where today I have ordered cakes. In a bag, he gave me a few sweets from one of the large jars with variously colored sweets that stood on the shop counter.

"For your good report," he said.

I stood stock-still, hardly daring to take the sweets. "What is the teacher doing behind the counter?" I asked myself. "Is he stealing the sweets perhaps? Should he be spending time in a baker's shop at all?" I couldn't bring myself to eat the sweets—I took them home to my mother.

I then began to overhear people talking about the young teacher and the baker's daughter. "He's carrying on brazenly with her," it was said, "but you just see—he'll drop her. He won't marry a baker's daughter."

Then I understood—partly at least—and ate up the sweets.

The mother of this girl—whom the teacher did marry—is still there behind the counter. She offers her condolences; I order the cakes, am spoken to by a woman who enters the shop after me.

Do I want the bells to be rung at the burial? she asks.

Certainly I do, but do I have to order that specially, and whom do I speak to?

She will see to it, and it costs ten marks. I press twenty marks into her hand. She takes the banknote silently and sticks it into her apron pocket.

# V

What we thought was humiliation you thought was a brilliant idea. You saved, kept your money together, wished to keep a close eye on all expenditures. We had a kind of account with the Woll sisters. We got no cash from them, but instead had a blue octavo notebook. Our purchases were written up in it. Hilda and Blondie copied what we needed to buy into the notebook. At the end of the month, you added everything up and paid with a check.

"Half a pound of margarine and a pound of flour," I would say, laying the notebook on the counter.

Hilda Woll nodded, licked her pencil stub, and wrote down the order. It was then entered into a second notebook that the Woll sisters kept safe in the drawer of the counter.

When the shop was closed, I had to go to Aunt Klärchen for shopping. There we had to pay cash.

"Please give me one mark, Daddy," I would say.

"Why?" you asked, surprised and annoyed.

"I must buy four eggs and two bits of cheese, otherwise we'll have nothing for supper."

"But your mother got five marks from me last week," you answered crossly. "What has happened to all that money?"

I was overcome with a guilty conscience and lowered my head, my heart thumping. By proxy. For I had not spent it for her on groceries, nor had it been blown on luxuries. You would have preferred to cancel the meal, because it signified to you nothing but unnecessary expense.

But for another reason, I really did have a guilty conscience. Boys from the village had found an air-force knife in good condition. It had been thrown away, along with many another things, when the troops had disbanded in the last days of the war. I was desperate to have it.

"Sell it to me," I said.

"You can have it for five marks," they said.

"Agreed," I said, "you'll get the money later." Without any further thought, I took the blue notebook to the Woll sisters and said, "I've come for five marks. Please write them down in the notebook." "Is it for your mother?" they asked.

I nodded uneasily.

Fortunately there was no other customer in the shop, for it always shamed me to death to have to produce the notebook. I gave the money to the boys and hid myself away with the knife in the attic.

Later I showed it to you and told you that I had found it in the forest.

"An air-force knife," you said. "The soldiers must have thrown it away when the Americans moved in. I hope you didn't find it in that place in the forest where all the ammunition is buried."

"No," I said, "I found it near Ausbacherhof."

"The knife is far too dangerous for him," said Mother.

You then put it on top of the kitchen cabinet, from where I would secretly take it down now and then and examine it fearfully.

Then the boys turned up again at the gate of the yard and hailed me.

"Can't we see the knife again?" they asked. I was afraid of them, and shook my head. "You're our friend," they said, "we'll buy it back from you."

"For how much?"

They conferred.

"For a bottle of cola."

I would much rather have kept the knife, but the boys were bigger than me, and I was afraid they would beat me up if I refused.

I nodded, fetched the knife from the kitchen cabinet, stuck it under my pullover, and carried it out. "You'll get the cola tomorrow," they said, and ran off.

I never got the cola.

At the end of the month the business over the five marks came out. There was a long argument about it, which I kept well out of.

"I know nothing about it," I said.

You accused Mother, swore at her. I never told you the truth, neither then nor later.

There was in fact money there to buy nice things. Because your suspenders had been repaired again and again, and in some places hung by only a few rubber threads, Mother gave you a new pair for your birthday, which she bought from Aunt Klärchen. I had to take the notebook to the Woll sisters to get the money, for you never gave her any ready cash.

When Mother beamingly handed you the suspenders with best wishes for your birthday, you went berserk. They were peasants' suspenders, you roared, they were as broad as a horse harness. And the old ones would be good for a long time yet. Mother had to return them to Aunt Klärchen and get back the money.

One day a man who lived in an almshouse and was supported—with his wife and six children—by the parish, brought a large basket of freshly picked raspberries. He wanted a mark for them. Would the Frau Doctor buy them from him? She took pity on him and told him she would send him the money as soon as you got back home. She was delighted, washed the raspberries, and was about to cook them. I still remember the scene she made, how she wept and wept. But I had to take them back to the man and say,

"My father says no." The man nodded and took the raspberries back. Without a word.

When the currency was reformed you got compensation in deutsche marks for the obsolete reichsmarks: a windfall, for we were living at the time in a converted sheepfold near Bremervörde, in which you also ran your medical practice. You were still wanted by the French, who had renewed their warrant for your arrest and were searching for you. The money could have paid for things that we really needed. My sister had just been born. The clothes that relatives had sent for me in gift parcels from America and Australia were too small. The cigarettes from those parcels served as exchange for the cod-liver oil that kept me alive.

You came back smiling from the district town—delayed, so it seemed. For the 945 new marks you had bought a high-quality microscope and two oil paintings showing the Devil's Moor near Worpswede. That was a better use of the money than on clothes that would soon get worn out, you explained.

Gone were the days when you had your uniform with the armband RFSS made by the best tailor in Berlin. You had rented at that time a furnished flat in the diplomatic quarter from a countess. You were still a bachelor, and your sister Anna ran the household. When your boss was invited to dinner with his wife, Frau Margarete Himmler, you had sent your sister out to buy flowers. She had to walk a long way, to a street where you knew a flower shop in which bouquets were considerably cheaper. You had your mother brought for this occasion from Einöllen. Next morning there was a huge parade. Your mother sat on the VIP stand, next to your erstwhile company commander, Rudolf Hess. For two days afterward your mother couldn't speak. She was speechless at the honor that had been paid to a farmer's wife from Einöllen. It didn't matter to you that her Sunday outfit—quite acceptable in church in

Einöllen—was somewhat out of place here. She didn't have the money for a new coat. She didn't need one, you said: for just one day in Berlin it would be an extravagance.

What to me was humiliation you thought was a brilliant idea. A castle in Hunsrück, built by one of your forebears, had become the Castle Hotel. You wanted to photograph it and were led round by the hotelier. You told me just to sit in the dining room and drink a lemonade. It was midday, and I sat down at the last free table.

The waiter put a menu in front of me. "I'm waiting for my father," I said, "please bring me a lemonade."

I studied the menu, whose prices seemed astronomical to me.

"Have you chosen anything yet?" asked the waiter, when he brought the lemonade. "No," I said, "I'll wait a bit longer, till my father comes."

Father was led outside by the hotelier, through the old rooms where the knights used to eat.

You proudly explained to the hotelier that one of our forebears had married the daughter of Johann von Eich, a government official from Kirchberg. And his great grandfather on his mother's side was the builder of the castle. "My son here," you said, pointing at me with a broad smile, for I had just edged up to you, "is therefore a direct descendant of the former owners of the castle." I was terribly embarrassed, tugged at your sleeve, and whispered: "I must order something to eat—the waiter has already come up to my table several times." You raised your eyebrows, took out your purse and gave me a five-mark piece. I went back to the table and studied the menu in terror.

The waiter returned.

"I'd like a fried egg with potatoes," I said hesitantly. It was the cheapest thing on the menu. It cost exactly five marks.

"A fried egg. Yes, Sir, surely," repeated the waiter.

I had the feeling that the whole dining room hurled back the echo of those words and that all the guests had been waiting to hear what I would order and were now watching me gleefully. I had not the slightest appetite, my mouth was all dried up, and I had to force the fried egg and boiled potatoes down.

I had the feeling that everyone was hanging over me and watching me. Me, in the clothes from the end-of-season sale, which I'd worn every day for many weeks and which looked baggy and ugly; stuck there for the first time as if on display before those noisy, elegant people; a fourteen-year-old boy unskilled with knife and fork. At home we never had guests. We never went to any social events, were never invited out, never ate in restaurants.

I remember the only occasion on which you broke out of this self-imposed isolation—for a few minutes. You had given the pastor of Einöllen a lift in your car. Previously you had always visited your patients by bicycle, but now you were driving again for the first time in your own car—a secondhand VW.

"Come, let's make our first trip, to the café at Wolfstein," you said.

The pastor was standing at the bus stop, waiting for the bus. He also wanted to go to the neighboring small town. You generously invited him to come too, proudly drank in his compliments on your new car.

Halfway there, the VW stalled. It wouldn't start again, though you went on pressing the starter for several minutes. Meanwhile the bus that the pastor wanted passed by. He nervously looked at his watch.

"It doesn't matter—it's not far from here, I can walk," he said kindly. He got out and wished us good luck.

I pushed the car to a downward stretch, where you could let it roll. You always switched off the engine and freewheeled down slopes to save gasoline.

You wanted to show the pastor how posh we were: that we had a car and he didn't.

———

You returned to my table with the hotelier. "Have you finished eating?" you asked. All I could do was nod.

"Good-bye, Herr Doctor," said the hotelier. "Good-bye, young man."

With knees trembling, I followed you out of the dining room. You had eaten nothing; you never ate anything on the trips we made, which were always to castles and fortresses that had previously belonged to some forebear of ours; you just had a cup of coffee. If coffee was available only in a pot, you would look at me and raise your eyebrows and adopt your typical expression: half ironic, half ashamed. I had the feeling that the high cost of the pot of coffee would bring us back to the breadline. My sister and I therefore just drank a lemonade, agreeing that we weren't hungry. Even when we were weak at the knees with hunger.

As we came down the steps of the Castle Hotel, you said cheerfully that the hotelier had been impressed that we were direct descendants of the builder of the castle. You thought that was brilliant too.

**6**

All the Gauchs in Einöllen were descended from Johann Jakob Gauch, who in 1731 married the daughter of the sheriff of the village. He was also the sheriff of half a dozen neighboring parishes and was described in the parish records as the richest farmer in the village and as a landowner. I tell this to my relatives as I go round now from house to house. My grandmother was herself born a Gauch; also my grandfather's mother. All the Gauchs, I say, are related to each other here.

Ute, my second cousin, has also married a Gauch from a distant branch of the family.

As a child I didn't know that so many people in the village were called Gauch. The families had assumed other names to distinguish themselves from each other. It was only made clear to me later, that the master tailor Adam Schneider was actually Adam Gauch, that Elsje Wagner was actually the wife of the cartwright Jacob Gauch, that my friend Willi Korb was really Willi Gauch, and that it was his grandmother who was born a Korb. Father was known as Peter's Herman because the house in which he was born was built by Peter Gauch.

I begin to recognize most of the faces. They were completely strange to me before; but now they belong to close relatives. I feel friendly toward these people for the first time—warmly so: I discover in them my father's features—his expression, his eyes, his hands. We work out all the relationships from a family album that my great-uncle brings from the front parlor into the kitchen.

"Your father became interested in the history of the family early on," said my great-uncle. "But not just in that. I recall how at Christmas once he organized a meeting here of the NSDAP. It was in 1923, and at that time no one actually knew anything about the Nazis. Most people here are Social Democrats—supporters of the SPD. The arguments were getting quite heated, and on New Year's Eve the SPD organized a meeting with their opponents and invited your father to a discussion. They had someone from town as a speaker—the editor of the newspaper there. He claimed that the Nazis really wanted the same policies as the centrists and the Communists: their program was just a con. Actually to put it into practice would mean another war."

"Was that already recognized, in 1923?" I ask in disbelief.

"Certainly, Sigfrid," said Uncle Jakob. "The newspaper had called the Nazis animals. Your father was a student then, in Munich, I think. And he was also at the same time fighting the separatists here. The French had circulated his description, made house-to-house searches for him."

"And later sentenced him to five years in prison," I added, "for terrorism."

My uncle stopped short. "It was all quite different then," he said. "One knew whom one was fighting against, one had the entire population of the Palatinate on one's side. And that sentence of five years—it was issued in his absence by a French military court. It was no longer recognized on the east side of the Rhine. So he was even free to practice as a doctor: the Red Cross set up an office for him, and later the sentence was in any case lifted under an amnesty."

I show my discomfiture; I say that it is awkward to be fond of one's father and yet to have utterly different political views from him.

"I could never discuss these things with him," I say. "When I was younger, he gave me long monologues; later, when he saw that I thought differently, he kept silent. Only in his last years, when he lived mainly in his memories, did he speak about them again; but I only listened because I wanted to understand him."

I feel especially staggered by the prophetic character of the 1923 meeting.

In the *People's Observer* of 6 January 1923 it was stated as follows: "Party member Gauch assured the meeting that the party could never and would never be the cause of a war with France. We were not allowed to put forward part of our evidence. But the sparks had been lit. The speaker for the Social Democrats collapsed into inarticulate embarrassment and denounced all our evidence as lies and our speaker as a liar; but he could not substantiate this, and instead called the leaders and members of our movement people of animal mentality and morals. He aroused in the audience—even in the rows of local Social Democrats—heckling and ridicule; but the speaker for the National Socialists was strongly applauded."

I wanted to know how the editor who was present as the speaker for the SPD reacted to this.

"He naturally let fly in his newspaper," said Uncle Jakob. "He said that your father would disrupt the whole region and that he too most probably had Jewish ancestors. That was perhaps why your father was so interested in family history!"

When Father started to talk about his past, it was mostly in cafés. Even later on, when we had moved to the town and I didn't have to go to the boarding school anymore, we would meet after school in a café. I had to translate Homer for him there, and he listened to my Latin vocab.

It didn't bother him at all that the other customers in the café could partake of my knowledge or ignorance. He couldn't see that I often had tears of anger or shame in my eyes, for his head was buried in the Latin grammar. He certainly noticed that I preferred to read Brecht and François Villon, Elias Canetti, and Peter Weiss; but he didn't react to that—he talked instead about what he himself had read in the past.

About how in just one semester in Cologne he had worked through the entire collection of books on Indo-European philology and then written an essay on runes; about how he read, while he was there, an article in the *Deutsche Zeitung* on a meeting in Munich: two sections of a hundred men had marched to protect it, carrying red flags with a Swastika on a white background and calling themselves the armed branch of the NSDAP.

"When was that?" I asked, glad to be able to distract him from vocab.

"In the late summer of 1922," he said.

Brecht was a student in Munich at that time, I reflected, and at the same time Father was a pupil at a gymnasium in Augsburg. Father was at the Saint Anna College; Brecht was at the *Realgymnasium*. "Did you not know Brecht?" I asked.

"I didn't know anyone in Augsburg," said Father tetchily, "for in my free time I did nothing but study. But when I read that article in Cologne, an inner voice said to me that this was the movement of the future.

"I packed my things and journeyed at the beginning of the semester to Munich. During the holidays I had got a job as a construction worker. I had to shift barrel loads of gravel all day, with the result that I developed tendonitis in one arm. The money that I earned and the disability benefits that I got for my arm condition were just enough for the train ticket to Munich."

"Did you meet Hitler there?" I asked.

"I did," said Father, casually, "but that came later. First I went along to the party office at 12 Corneliusstrasse. I showed them my construction worker's identity card and asked them if they would take me. I was actually only a part-time worker, and I thought a workers party was only for workers! They laughed and said that as a student I also had to work."

"And then you met Hitler?" I asked again.

"Yes, at the next meeting," he said. Father's voice was quite loud, and the people who were sitting at the next table in the café had long since stopped talking. They pretended to be interested in the view outside the window and placed their coffee cups very lightly on their saucers. Father noticed nothing of this.

"I was assigned to the second hundred-strong section of the SA—the Sturmabteilung, which had only just been set up," he said. "Hitler spoke in the large room at the Hofbräuhaus. I was deployed on the staircase to the room and was told to let no one else come up, for the room had already been closed off by the police because of overcrowding. An old man wanted to push past me. I started to tussle with him because he wouldn't give in—till he said: 'I am Dietrich Eckart.'" Father smiled to himself at the memory.

"And who was he?" I asked.

Father looked surprised and annoyed; I felt a cramp in my stomach and felt guilty.

"Don't you know? What do you actually learn at school? Eckart was a writer and editor of the *People's Observer.*"

That interested me little. "And Hitler?" I asked.

"I came into personal contact with Hitler in December 1922," said Father. "He had a speech to give in Göppingen. When he was leaving he directed those of us who were deployed to protect the hall to report to him again at a pub in Munich. He went from one to the other, shook hands with each of us, and looked me so directly in the eye that I felt quite peculiar. He then said to us: 'It's going to be hard for us this evening, and if anyone flinches in the slightest, I shall personally rip off his badge!'"

"And in Göppingen?" I ask.

The people at the next table looked frequently at their watches but made no move to depart. Father was in full flight now, but I didn't dare ask him to speak more quietly.

"The Communists were already being transported to Göppingen by truck; at the eleventh hour the meeting was banned by the

Württemberg authorities. We consequently marched up the other side of the Donau to hold an evening of discussion. On the way to the bridge we were attacked by the Communists with cobblestones, and when we were on the bridge they began to shoot. Mercilessly. The wounded and the nurses attending them were deliberately singled out. An SA man who was running beside me to the left was shot in the chest; the man on my right was shot in the leg."

"Didn't the police move in?" I wanted to know.

"Ah, the police," said my father. "They just shouted at us from a distance: 'In the name of the law. . . .' As the one with the most experience of military service, I had to take command of the section. It consisted mostly of students because it was easier for them to spare time for such activities than it was for workers. I took control of our defense until police from three towns moved in and took us to the railway station.

"They let us leave unhindered, but we were arrested in Ulm and charged with disturbing the peace. They had us thoroughly searched for weapons, but I had strapped my pistol onto my belly. Because they didn't find it, I was released from the charge of 'forming an armed gang.'"

"At that time the Palatinate was under French rule," I said. "That didn't cause you any difficulties?"

"What do you mean by difficulties?" asked Father ironically in return. "We fought incessantly against the separatists, organized strikes on the railways, unscrewed railway sleepers in order to derail their transport trains, and went through the customs controls on the Rhine illegally with forged papers.

"I went about most of the time with all my war weapons: pistols, ammunition, and hand grenades. In addition, I smuggled forged papers and was deployed as a courier. The occupying French troops consisted almost always of colonial soldiers who only spoke broken French. So I always passed myself off as

French—they didn't notice my accent—and got through the controls that way. But once all my talking in French didn't help me: a sentry became suspicious. I had to open my suitcase: my dirty washing and personal possessions lay on the top, but it was full of weapons underneath. The sentry started to take everything out piece by piece, and I considered whether I should seize his weapon from him and shoot him. He soon had in his hand the first-aid packs that we always needed after fistfights or gunfights.

"'*Qu'est-ce que c'est que ça?*' he asked.

"I answered, 'Those are first-aid packs, which as a doctor I always have to carry.' '*Vous êtes médecin?*' he asked respectfully, and when I said '*Oui, monsieur,*' he snapped my suitcase shut."

"Weren't you also there when the president of the Palatinate was shot?" I asked.

"Not at the shooting itself," said Father. "Volunteers were used for that. As non-Rhinelanders they had to face the death sentence that we had evaded. Eight of us had met beforehand—at the end of 1923—at a hotel, the Heidelberger Hof in Heidelberg: that was where we worked out the plan for shooting him. But first my brother Karl was sent to set fire to his farmhouse in Orbis, as a fiery foretaste, so to speak. He bound his head with a white bandage and spattered it with chicken blood. Then he rode by bicycle into the farm—the home of the president of the so-called Autonomous Government of the Palatinate—and told the president's sister that he had been beaten up by the Nazis and that he was one of her brother's supporters. She took him in and offered him a bed for the night. But he said he would rather sleep in the hay in the barn—he would be safer there from the volunteers. During the night he set fire to the farm and fled."

Father was beaming. He was rarely as lively and talkative as this. Now and then I looked nervously around me, expecting someone at the next table to jump up in a rage. But in the Palatinate these stories still seemed to give pleasure. "In the description that the French circulated," said Father, "it was said that my brother Karl had a small face, very blond hair, blue eyes, small hands, and manicured fingernails; that he spoke High German and was probably a student.

"Heinz-Orbis, the president, prophesied after the fire that the bullet for him had already been cast. He was right. Two of the volunteers died in the attack, but Heinz-Orbis died too. But tell me, in case you forget: Does the verb in a subordinate clause in a sentence that is in the past take the imperfect or pluperfect subjunctive?"

The people at the next table called out to the waiter to bring the bill.

I say nothing in Einöllen about my contradictory feelings during my school years. I had, after all, a father who had experienced more than those other fathers who were an object of pride to their sons, whose social standing led to a kind of pecking order in the class at the gymnasium, even though I was not aware of that then. I had a father who had experienced more than other fathers; but none of those experiences could be spoken about.

I struggle to suppress those thoughts again. On the way home from Einöllen I pass through Meisenheim. I do not look at all at the windows of the boarding school, which must now be brightly lit; the separate buildings have probably been developed into an elaborate complex. My eyes are stocked instead with the faces and gestures of my relatives in Einöllen, together with the image of my father.

# VI

On 1 September 1939 you again volunteered for military service—with the Luftwaffe this time. You were in the army in the First World War, in the marines in the twenties. All the uniforms that were worn by the various Nazi organizations were already hanging in your closet. You were eager to learn to fly. But during your flying lessons, after five flights, when you wanted to conquer the heavens by flying alone in a glider, you handled the landing so clumsily that the glider was smashed—and you were made unfit for flying by smashing your fourth vertebra.

You became a military doctor in Lauterecken, not far from your home village.

On 13 October German fighters shot down their first British plane: it had strayed by mistake into the Palatinate's airspace on its way back to Britain after a reconnaissance flight. The Blenheim caught fire and plunged down over Langweiler, not far from Lauterecken.

You were informed by telephone and rushed to the crash site with your driver and a soldier. The plane had a crew of three. The parachutes of two of them had caught fire, and they had fallen to the ground like stones; the third was alive. He landed in a tree. Farmers had cut him out of his parachute and brought him to the village in a horse-drawn cart. He was an officer, a wing commander with the Royal Air Force, and had serious burns on his face and hands.

He stared at you with terror. You were the first German officer he had seen, and he expected perhaps to be liquidated by your armed driver. You introduced yourself to him in your school English as a Luftwaffe doctor and explained that he was a prisoner of war. You spoke respectfully, of course, to a fellow officer. You ordered a burial with military honors for the two dead soldiers.

You gave medical attention to the wing commander: covered his burns with emergency bandages and carried him away in your car. You sat in front, next to the driver; the wing commander sat at the back next to the armed soldier.

The wing commander was terrified again.

You halted in Fischbach-Weierbach in Hunsrück district. It was the last place before Idar-Oberstein, where there were large barracks with a military hospital: you wanted to leave your first prisoner of war there.

Your cousin had a practice in Fischbach-Weierbach. Together, you treated his burns professionally and then opened a bottle of wine. Officers together: your cousin was a staff doctor too, in the nearby military hospital. One bottle was not enough, even though you normally drank only fruit juice and sipped at a glass of the wine merely out of politeness.

Meanwhile you informed the commandant of the military hospital. You told him you had a British officer. The German officer came personally to fetch his prisoner. He introduced himself as Hubertus, Prince of Prussia, grandson of the last Kaiser, descendant of Queen Victoria, and a cousin of the king of England.

Wing Commander Harry M. A. Day, the first officer of the Royal Air Force to be taken as a prisoner of war (on his first operational flight), no longer understood the world. It began to wobble before his eyes, for the wine was good.

When toward evening you politely indicated—officer to officer—that it was time to leave, Wing Commander Day asked pleasantly, "Am I going to a hotel now?"

He went to the barracks, but life in the officers' mess was quite tolerable.

The junior German officers were very excited and roared out, "If things go on like this, the Führer will personally fetch the king of England as a prisoner of war."

Wing Commander Day felt duty bound—as the longest-held prisoner of war—to organize feats of heroism. Coming as he did from a famous military family, it was a disgrace to have been captured on his first military mission. He continually organized escape attempts, which were mostly unsuccessful. When he once did manage to break out, he was relieved to be picked up again after two days.

He was sent to more and more heavily guarded camps—to Dachau and Sachsenhausen. He was always the "Father of the Camp" and was treated well. He got to know Stalin's son, who was also a prisoner, and the plotters against Hitler of 20 July 1944. He saw their bodies being carted past his cell window on wheelbarrows after their execution, the piano wire that had strangled them still around their necks.

Thirty years later he stood outside your door, having sent you a letter of thanks for "the humane treatment I received when I was shot down." You had used this letter as exoneration material during the denazification proceedings. One of his wartime comrades—the editor of *Paris Match* after the war—wrote a book about him. Three years previously he had come to see you while researching it, and I had driven him through the area, to the crash site at Langweiler and then to Fischbach-Weierbach, to the family of your now dead cousin. I interpreted, and he made notes. He noted down the label of a bottle of wine that was served to us in Fischbach-Weierbach. It crops up in the book on Wing

Commander Day—backdated by thirty years: Deidesheimer Linsenbusch 1937.

The wing commander stood before your door, introduced himself, and explained that he wanted to celebrate the thirtieth anniversary of his shooting down over Langweiler. He stayed for afternoon coffee, and we didn't know what to offer to him. You had nothing in the house to eat.

In a corner of a kitchen drawer we found some old, dried-up tea bags. "The English always drink tea," I said, and brewed some up.

It tasted disgusting, not only to me.

Would the wing commander prefer something else? I asked. He wouldn't mind a glass of wine, he answered.

I asked you for money and hurriedly bought a bottle in the nearby corner shop, which was run by a male couple. I also bought a little bottle of whiskey—a sample bottle that I'd noticed on the shelf.

The English always drink whiskey, I thought. The wing commander looked at the bottle and shook his head. I rinsed out a toothbrush glass and offered him the wine. No one drank with him. He sat stiffly and drank to our health.

You reminisced and wanted to show him a passage in a book. "Unfortunately I can't find the book at the moment," you said.

"Oh that's no problem," I said. "It must be here on the bottom shelf."

"It doesn't matter," you said. "Leave it." But I was already combing through the bookcase and soon pulled the book out.

"Leave it now," he said, somewhat louder. "It's not in that one."

I continued to search, and when you told me even more loudly to stop looking I understood: the books that were suddenly lying on the floor of the living room had bright red covers and thick black swastikas in white circles.

With a quick side glance at the wing commander—who was still thinking about the exact proportion of sugar to vinegar in the wine he had just drunk and had noticed nothing—I hurriedly shoved the subversive pile of books back into the bookcase.

Your expression was black. You'd been made to look stupid.

The wing commander declined to have his glass topped up. He drove on to Fischbach-Weierbach, where he was received with more hospitality.

On 13 October of the following year he turned up again. He said that he wanted to celebrate the thirty-first anniversary of his shooting down.

This time he stayed in a hotel and invited us there. He chose the wine in the restaurant. You sipped at it politely. You were less taciturn than usual and dug out your school English again.

In the book about Day you are described as "an elderly, kindly man" who spoke "in strongly accented English."

On 13 October of the following year Wing Commander Day arrived yet again. He said that he wanted to celebrate the thirty-second anniversary of his shooting down. But this time in grand style.

The whole of Langweiler was assembled there: the district magistrate and the pastor; representatives of the French, British, and American military attachés; the German air marshal who was in charge of the former barracks.

There were speeches of remembrance and thanks. "When I was brought down on your land," said the wing commander, "I did indeed expect to be treated correctly, but more with military discipline than with friendly warmth."

You were one of the guests of honor. You opened up and spoke as much as you had in the entire year.

The wing commander had had engraved on a plaque the names of those he remembered with particular affection. Among them was the name of a concentration camp doctor with whom he had become friendly. For you this was proof that the treatment in the concentration camps was correct and all the talk about the Holocaust was lies.

Your name too was engraved.

You were the center of attention: photographed, mentioned. "This is my son, a reserve officer," you said with shining eyes to the air marshal when you introduced me to him.

You had taken me by the arm and said, "Come along, I want to introduce you to the air marshal."

You joined the group that was chatting with the air marshal. You stood there like a schoolboy who has something important to say to his teacher and can't bear to wait for his turn. You gazed up at the air marshal, who was more than a head taller than you, and your voice trembled. "This is my son," you said, "he is a reserve officer."

The air marshal smiled wearily. We struggled to exchange polite, incidental remarks. You were pleased, very pleased.

The following year—and the year after that—the family nervously asked you as early as September if you had heard anything from Wing Commander Day.

Then when postcards arrived in handwriting that was nearly illegible because of Parkinson's disease—from Kent or from Malta—plans were hastily hammered out.

Who was ready to volunteer this year? Who would be driver?—as requested by the air-force barracks, where the wing commander expected a car and driver to be at his service.

Our ridicule and unwillingness were offensive to you. You looked forward to these visits. For then you were again the Senior Staff Doctor, Retired, present with the British Wing Commander, Retired, among smart uniforms. Among people.

Each year, when Harry M. A. Day turned up for his anniversary on 13 October, his Parkinson's disease was worse. A third double whiskey was no longer sufficient to stop the trembling in his hands.

———

The last year that the wing commander celebrated his shooting down, you and my wife were invited to the best hotel in the town. I was engaged elsewhere, and you had—exceptionally—agreed to my wife's being present.

Mr. Day came with an American lady friend of his, and a dinner table for four had been booked.

Wine was drunk—lots of wine—and you sipped a glass out of politeness.

It should have been an official wine-tasting session! The wing commander was in a good mood, and he took his lady friend through the various wine regions. If she didn't like one, he would tip the glass empty over his shoulder onto the hotel curtains.

He slipped money to the harmonium player to persuade him to play old air-force marches. He wanted to show you how well he still knew English marching steps. He led you onto the long red carpet in the middle of the dining room.

The guests at the neighboring table had come with women. He knew all about women, said the wing commander. He took the yellow carnations that decorated the table out of their vase and presented them to the women at the other tables. He dropped down onto his knee and acted the perfect cavalier.

In the end, the three of you had to carry the American woman to a taxi.

The next year a card came saying that his old car had broken down and he couldn't come. That was almost like Christmas for us. We heard no more of him after that.

By chance I heard from a friend that the ZDF wanted to make a film of this story. The friend had been told this in confidence, and—assuming I was to be the scriptwriter—congratulated me. I had earlier given him a detailed account of the whole business.

You had discovered that the son-in-law of your cousin in Fischbach-Weierbach—a TV writer—was writing it. But you took no further interest: it had become a matter of indifference to

you. You now lived only in the past, spoke of how you had to initial documents in Berlin with a red pen that in status came directly below the green pen of the minister. That was the time you had
a made-to-measure, olive-green suit with sewn-on pockets. Your
last uniform.

# 7

"Free yourself of him," said Herbert on the telephone when he heard about Father's death.

Herbert has lived for forty years in London. He had not yet left Germany when Father was called to Berlin by Walther Darré, Heinrich Himmler, Rudolf Hess, and Alfred Rosenberg. I feel exhausted this evening after all my conversations in Einöllen: no appetite. I have a desire to talk to someone who can see our recent history from a different perspective.

Herbert is the same age that Father was when the war ended and has rejected the idea of returning. He was offered lucrative posts, such as the directorship of a research institute, but he preferred to stay self-employed in London on a very low income.

"Your father," says Herbert, "thought he was one of those great idealists who believe in what they say or write. But in reality he was an obdurate, unreformable Nazi till the day he died."

I do not rebut this.

"This sounds hard today, my dear friend," says Herbert, "but don't forget: at that time there were other Germans. In Berlin, over four thousand Jews *survived* the Nazis' reign of terror; in Berlin! survived the whole war! They were hidden in flats, in attics, and it wasn't only they who lived in constant fear of death: the people in whose houses they lived—on whose miserable ration cards they depended—suffered the same fear."

"Yes," I say softly, "fear of that death in which my father was complicit."

It does me good to hear Herbert's voice, even though he does not lessen the guilt that I feel: guilt by proxy.

At the end of 1933 Father was a doctor with the marines. He had been obliged to give up again the general practice that, after his sentence under French military law, the German Red Cross gave him as part of the aid program for citizens of the Rhine-Ruhr. He was also active—in the area around Bremen—as a speaker and propagandist for the Nazis.

A newspaper wrote in 1926 that the small place where he lived "was distinguished by the presence of some notable Swastika Wearers; and if that is not enough, there is a Dr. Gauch—a school doctor paid by the Prussian state—who has been no less contaminated with nationalism."

So his position as a marine officer did not stop him from continuing his political campaigning: as a party speaker, as a contributor to student magazines. Because he was also a contact man for the SA and gave the party reports on internal naval matters, the politically neutral marines wanted to charge him in 1933 with high treason.

"At the end of 1933," said Father on his last birthday, "the Third Reich government came to us at Kiel, and I conversed with several party leaders and ministers, especially Darré (the Minister for Agriculture), with Rosenberg, Ammler, and Rudolf Hess, my first SA company commander."

They had spontaneously offered him an advisory post, and he thus went to work for Darré in Berlin as the director of the Ethnology Department.

Your place of work was soon afterward moved from the agri-culture ministry to the Gestapo headquarters in Prinz-Albrecht-Strasse, where the room of the commandant of the Führer's body-guard had become free.

"But the telephone on my desk remained directly connected with the Reich chancellery," said Father proudly, "and I signed the documents with a red pen, which in status came immediately below the green pen of the minister.

"We formed a circle of offices round Himmler's room: Hey-drich, the police adjutant, the bodyguard adjutant, and I. Himm-ler recognized me as his adjutant on cultural and political affairs.

"All I can say is that the aims that were declared were impec-cable," Father stressed after more than half a century. "Darré said to me, 'You occupy my most important post.'"

"So you were in the Prinz-Albrecht-Strasse, were you?" I asked.

Father understood my question at once. "It's all bogus, what has been written about it. I used to go in and out of that building; had there been screams of torture from the basement, I would certainly have heard. But I never heard any screaming. And when I visited SD Führer Dr. Best down there, I heard nothing.

"One of my friends, the Reverend von Schweinitz from Meisenheim, was taken into that cellar for a whole night—and was then set free. The information he had given was merely checked; nothing was done to him."

"But you were only there from 1933 to 1935," I said, "not later."

"Ah, but none of what is written today is true," said Father angrily. "It's a falsification of history. Read the letters that SS Gen-eral Pohl wrote me from Landsberg Prison; he was hanged after the Nuremberg trials for being in charge of the Warsaw Ghetto. Even from his death cell, he wrote that it was all lies.

"Before 1933 I asked Frick, the future Minister of the Inter-ior, what would be done with the Communists on our coming to power. He said that they would all be rounded up into camps to stop them from causing a disturbance."

"So now you're admitting it yourself!" I said.

"What do you mean?" shouted Father, aroused by a double Euphyllin injection. "These horror stories about the concentration camps are pack of lies!

"Someone from our village was deployed as an SS guard in the concentration camp at Mauthausen. After the war, when he had gone underground as a laborer near Bremen, where I started up my practice again, we went together to one of the films that the Americans were showing to the Germans. It was allegedly about the survivors of the concentration camps. The SS guard suddenly burst out, "I know him, and him too—they are German soldiers!" Half-starving German prisoners of war were passed off as former inmates of concentration camps.

"And the whole idea of the Jewish extermination was cooked up by the quarter-Jew Heydrich, who wanted thereby to hush up the fact that his own grandmother was Jewish.

"Heydrich was with the marines, together with me and Pohl; it was already known there that he had Jewish ancestry. Himmler asked me one day if I believed these rumors, and I told him that it had long been known within the marines. But he came one day and said that Heydrich had explained everything to him: it had been the second wife of his grandfather, Süss by name. But Himmler then said that Süss didn't have to be a Jewish name, and one only had to look at Heydrich, fair-haired German that he was. So trustful was Himmler that he believed what Heydrich said!

"But Heydrich had his nephew as an adjutant—with the same name—and he had his room behind Heydrich. I would guess that he helped him with his genealogy. When Heydrich was forced to make a complaint about a slur from a party comrade about his Jewish descent, the relevant page was missing from the parish registry, and his grandparents' gravestone in Magdeburg had also vanished. But I know this only from hearsay.

"Pohl, who had given information about Heydrich to Himmler, wrote from his very death cell that it was tragic that the quarter-Jew Heydrich—of all people—had been the intellectual initiator of this genocide. Canaris was the one who had acquired documents about Heydrich's ancestry from the marines; he and Pohl were therefore in a position to blackmail him. And only after Heydrich was murdered could Canaris—who had been protected by him—be arrested."

Father would break off discussions like this abruptly. He was out of breath, his lips were turning blue, his eyes were red and glassy. He would take an inhaler out of his jacket pocket and spurt its contents into his mouth. I felt that I had fallen into an abyss or was watching some kind of sinister film: felt as I did when the Eichmann trial was on and Father sent Eichmann's defense counsel Pohl's letters from Landberg as exoneration material.

Oswald Pohl, who had risen from being senior purser with the marines to a top administrative position with the SS, was still describing Father in 1950 from his death cell as his "dear, true friend"; wrote of his "vigor and helpfulness," and of how "there had at these trials been enough perjury under oath to fill a hundred years." Father had, wrote Pohl, "seen more deeply and clearly than those whose ambition drove them to commit crimes—a fact that had not been recognized at the time"; and before his execution in 1951 Pohl wrote, "Do you think we would improve the world and alter our fate if we told them now what kind of swine the others were? We would not thereby expunge from the world the great genocide that we engineered in the stupidest fashion against the Jews."

While the trial went on, Father had meetings at autobahn rest stops with Nazi survivors (including the widow of a concentration camp commandant), shook off real or imaginary pursuers, and carried a loaded pistol in his trouser pocket.

When the newspapers all reported that the chief prosecutor in the Eichmann trial described Father as one of the desk murderers responsible for what had happened, for days on end he no longer went out of the house.

"The Israeli Secret Service will hunt me down and kill me now," he said.

I could understand why Herbert became too angry to laugh on evenings when we met and talked in pubs in the Hampstead area of London.

"How did the other Nazis react to him?" he asked. "Did Himmler feel able to keep him?"

"No," I said, "he quarreled with everyone. For Darré he drew up a calendar reform in which all Christian festivals were to be replaced with old German ones, so that even the future Pope Pius XII, who had just agreed to the concordat with the Reich, protested. For Himmler he created a memorial grove at Verden-on-the-Aller for the Saxons who had been killed by Kaiser Karl, and wanted to introduce the official title Karl the Slaughterer—as a result of which he fell out with the historians. Darré applied for a professorship for him that was turned down, and he dealt with his official business in the Prinz-Albrecht-Strasse from a nearby café: his staff had to bring documents there for his signature.

"After a few months he had to withdraw and return to his medical practice in the Palatinate. In 1939 he volunteered again for the armed forces—for the Luftwaffe. Yet in his books—which were prescribed as textbooks in schools—he tried to make out that the Nordic race was the end product of Creation!"

Although I was afraid—with every additional word—that I might lose Herbert's friendship, I carried on talking: I had to carry on. I had to let him know how all this preyed on my mind, oppressed me.

"And worst of all, Herbert: many of his theories have received pseudoconfirmation from certain obscure researchers in England and America, who want to create a 'higher breed' of human being through gene manipulation: that was Father's idea some fifty years ago. The *Jewish Daily Bulletin* wrote in 1934 about his book, *New Foundations for Racial Research:* 'Nazi pseudoscientist finds newest "missing link" in Jews.'

"He distinguished between the Nordic and non-Nordic races, and wrote that the non-Nordic type was a halfway stage between the Nordic and the ape. The non-Nordic was therefore not actually a human being distinct from animals but only a bridge, an intermediate stage, for which one had to use the term *Untermensch.*"

Herbert laughed no more. He drank more than usual and was subdued. Drops of sweat stood out on his pale chin. He began to chew his fingernails—something he never normally did. "A genetic theory that teaches that there are differences between races—isn't it just a justification for racial extermination?" he asked. "Haven't talentless people thereby tried to get rid of the more gifted out of impotent envy and rivalry?"

I offered no direct answer. "Even when he boasted," I said, "that in his book he had never once used the word *Jew,* it was actually the basis of this whole genocidal madness." And after a pause: "And this is the superego with which I have to live."

"Rubbish," responded Herbert angrily, "*you* don't have to live with it; *he* has to. Why don't you try to live with the other Germans who were there? During the pogrom of 1938, which has been trivialized so elegantly with the term *Reichskristallnacht,* a horde of SA people stormed our home in Berlin, broke the door down, and wanted to take my father away—who, by chance, was out that evening. While they threatened and interrogated my family, my mother secretly called from the next room to one of our friends, who was an inspector with the police, an opponent of the Nazis—also, by the way, an opponent of the Communists. Later the Nazis put him into a concentration camp, and after the war the Russians imprisoned him too.

"When he came into the room, those thugs were pressing a pistol against my chest (I was only a small boy then) and threatening,

'If you won't say where your father is, we'll shoot you.' But I truly had no idea where he was! It was only when they started to smash up all our furniture that our friend managed to cow them by pulling his police rank, and sent them packing.

"Eight days later we were warned that they were out to arrest us and we should flee. We went to the door of the police inspector's flat: all of us—the whole family. He understood at once what was afoot and turned white as chalk, for if we were discovered this would also mean the end for him and his family. But he let us in without a word, and kept us there until we were able to cross the border and come to England.

"Try to live with people like that and forget stories your father told, such as the one about the Jewish ancestry of the SS bigwig Heydrich. If Heydrich was 'a quarter Jewish,' then one might as well believe that the Jews murdered themselves. By clinging to such stories," said Herbert, "you yourself are in danger of trying to construct excuses, of imagining that there might be justifications."

When I telephone Herbert this evening, we exchange only a few sentences about my father. "Free yourself of him," he says. Then he speaks of mutual acquaintances, and we laugh about them.

# *VII*

You were a father on weekends.

You said that you would be there at three o'clock. At exactly three o'clock we saw your Volkswagen through the window, waiting close to the house. We hurried to get ready, for you were impatient. But you never told us off: not once did you say, "Hurry up! I'm waiting."

After four minutes, you started up the car and drove ten meters farther on.

After another four minutes you drove another ten meters.

We ran up to you and said, "Good morning." You nodded. "Where are we going?" I asked.

"To Sponheim Castle," you answered.

You told us that the counts of Sponheim were our ancestors. Johann II, the count of Sponheim-Kreuznach, was the father of Walrab von Koppenstein—whose mother was the wife of an official in the castle. Because she was not of the same rank, their sons were merely barons. That was the castle we were going to today. You showered us with dates and their genealogical connection with us.

But we were more interested in who should sit next to you and who should take the back seat. Gudrun would not give way, but I was older and stronger. We got more and more vociferous:

during the journey we struggled to squeeze into the back seat and take each other's places.

When you finally told us off—"Why can't you just sit still?"— we fell as quiet as mice. Neither of us spoke anymore. Gudrun clambered into the space behind the back seat and stayed there. She knew that I, having angered you, would be too scared now to say anything more for the rest of the journey while she could make faces with impunity.

The wait till the evening, for my chance to slap her in revenge, was like an eternity.

We had to pose together in front of Sponheim Castle, which consisted of only a few bits of wall. You took your Leica out of one trouser pocket and an exposure meter out of the other. The sun had to be behind you.

"Look this way," you said, and we had to look into the bright sunlight. My eyes were streaming, but I tried not to blink. Then you lowered the camera to adjust the focus.

"Look at me," you said, and we had to stare into the sunlight again.

Then you lowered the camera again and examined the exposure meter. You fixed the correct exposure, and told us to look once more.

We had to stare into the bright sunlight again and didn't dare to wipe a single tear from our blinded eyes.

We didn't know when the shutter would click and didn't move.

Then you lowered the camera yet again and checked the distance, aperture, and shutter speed to make sure.

"Ready now!" you shouted as we grimaced with pain. You now aimed the camera. You held it very calmly, breathed in deeply, and breathed out half the air. You then held your breath and pressed the shutter. "That's it," you said breezily, not noticing our half-blinded eyes.

You took a small piece of paper out of your doctor's bag and noted down the number of the exposure, the date, and the place. It took about a year to use up a whole roll of film. But over time, in the photo albums accumulated many photos of castles with two grimacing children in front.

Eventually we would find an inn and drink a lemonade. You ordered a cup of coffee and told the landlord that we were descendants of the counts of Sponheim. I would have preferred the landlord to know nothing about that, for I had long grown out of my trousers and jacket; they were baggy and patched, and there were holes in my shoes. Gudrun's dress was far too short.

You proudly showed us, around that time, the newspapers in which there were essays by you on the counts of Sponheim—sometimes with poems alongside attributed to Gudrun and me. We once had to hide Gudrun when a married couple from the next town turned up, wanting to meet the gifted young poetess.

Gudrun was just seven years old. You had written the poem yourself.

The pupils at the secondary modern school once had to learn one of "my" poems, which celebrated my birthplace. "I greet thee, O happy town!" it began. You had written the poem and thought it would please me.

About a fortnight ago I was quizzed on one of these poems after it had been reprinted in a local annual. "Was it a youthful folly?" I was asked.

> *Although your walls are fallen down,*
> *Although your tower is rubble,*
> *Your holy blood still lives in us:*
> *It still, like you, is noble!*

Or

> *German people, in whose veins*
> *Noble blood is flowing,*
> *Let your great grandsires be praised*
> *While our sons are growing!*

One day a letter came from Hans Ulrich Rudel, the Luftwaffe officer for whom Hitler specially created a variation of the Knight's Cross with diamonds and swords and oak leaves. He thanked me for the beautiful poem in which I had extolled him and his deeds.

You were disappointed that I was not delighted by this. Your face was contorted with anger when you found out that I had written to Rudel, thanking him for his letter but telling him that you had written the poem. I didn't know that this poem too had been printed with my name beneath it.

For a while you were not able to be a father even on weekends. A grown-up dragged me by the hand through the town, and I saw your face behind the plateglass window of a café. You looked out at me, and I would have gladly run to you, embraced you; I would have gladly wept and let you take me in your arms. I didn't cry till the evening, under the bedclothes. I pressed my head into the pillow so that my sobbing could not be heard.

You had at that time explained to me how to make a collect call. With thumping heart I said to the post office clerk that I wanted to make a collect call. The post office was just by the primary school, and on the way home I had sometimes been there before. But I was frightened this time of being laughed at by the clerk. Maybe one couldn't make a collect call there, I thought.

I heard the clerk saying into the receiver: "Will you accept a collect call?" Then he sent me into the next cabin, and I heard your voice.

One day your sister picked up the phone. She had just come back from Africa, where she had lived for many years. She had never heard of collect calls, and when the clerk asked her if she would accept one, she answered, "A collect call? What would I do with that?" "I'm sorry," said the clerk, "the call was not accepted."

I believed that you had refused it.

I ran home distraught, hid in the orchard, pressed my face into the grass, and howled.

---

We had at the time accounts at two shops in the village where my sister and I lived: at the confectioner and at the greengrocer. We bought chocolate and bananas and said, "Daddy will pay." We had to eat them secretly on the way home, for no one was supposed to know, apart from you and us.

You came on weekends and paid.

We did not make full use of these accounts, for we were ashamed to buy without paying.

Soon afterward I started at the boarding school.

Every morning we were given a slice of bread for a snack, wrapped in greaseproof paper. The slices were lugged into the dining room from the kitchen in large baskets and shared.

I stuck my slice into my satchel and let it stay there. I couldn't eat it, even though I was so hungry. It nauseated me. Even today I have to find excuses if I say among friends, "I wouldn't mind a bite to eat now," and one of them pulls out a wrapped-up slice of bread and says, "There's real, homemade liver sausage on it."

When the satchel was full, and the bread—though hard as stone by then—began to stink, I stuffed it at the beginning of break under my pullover, ran to the toilets, and got rid of it there. I must have collected hundreds of slices of bread in greaseproof paper during my time at the boarding school.

But I eagerly devoured the bread that you kept in your room. A white French loaf was there, and half a ring of liver sausage. When I was alone in your room, I would secretly cut thin slices of bread, smear them sparingly with liver sausage, and eat them with fear and intense pleasure. I was afraid that you would be hungry if I ate too much. I knew that white bread with liver sausage was at that time your only sustenance. A long white loaf and half a pound of sausage lasted you several days. You took a cup of coffee in the Town Hall Café while listening to my vocabulary.

---

This was why I was often afraid of eating up someone's food. The rolls given me by the Hinterberger family, for example. Herr Hinterberger was one of your few decent acquaintances. For a few years after 1945 he wasn't allowed to teach in a school and therefore gave me some coaching for free. After the lessons—which I enjoyed and which really did improve my performance—Frau Hinterberger would come with fresh rolls, butter, jam, and hot cocoa. Sheer heaven! But I usually said I wasn't hungry.

I'm being coached for free, I thought to myself, so how can I eat up all their food as well?

A little while ago, Frau Hinterberger—now eighty years old—wrote, "One day your dear father came to have a button sewn on. I asked him to take off his coat. After a lot of persuasion he did so, and then I saw that his whole coat lining was torn. I lovingly repaired the whole coat, and how delighted he was!"

All of this seemed normal to me, and I had no idea that it could have been different.

At this time, you were my father on weekends.

# 8

Even this morning I need an alarm clock. I thought on the day of Father's burial that I would be lying awake at dawn, but the wine yesterday evening sent me so deeply asleep that I don't even remember dreaming.

My black suit has become a bit tight. When I bought it, I thought, One day I shall wear it at Father's funeral—and was instantly shocked by my thought. I drink coffee and read the newspaper as I do every morning. But instead of driving to school, I drive to the local florist to pick up the funeral wreath.

"A wreath like this has never been seen in this village before," says the florist as he proudly carries it to my car.

It consists of laurel and more than three hundred yellow roses. My first tears start to trickle now down my sideburns. "I shall start to sob," I say, and the florist tries to reassure me: I don't need to feel ashamed—it was just the same with him when his mother died.

This annoys me, for I am not at all ashamed. I am just surprised that it has happened here, on buying yet again a present for Father that he doesn't need.

The grave is fully dug, and the morgue is open. In the small room into which the coffin will be transferred shortly before the burial, there are dozens of wreaths. They are stacked up next to each other; on each one, a card is tied with wire.

I open some of the cards; they are mostly signed "Gauch" or "Gauch by birth." Card after card, they have the same format: "Sincere condolences." Wreath after wreath, they are identical. All the wreaths have been ordered from the local florist: fir-tree twigs with a bouquet of plastic flowers. The only exceptions are the wreaths from Munich, Frankfurt, and Bremen. I take note of the fact that no wreath is as big and beautiful as the one I have brought. I place it directly in front of the coffin.

It is icy cold in the morgue. We still have over an hour to go to visit the dying Aunt Klärchen. Her sister, who looked so fresh and blooming at the church fete, looks thin and careworn: she has been at Klärchen's bedside night after night.

"No change at all," she says. "Would your children like to see her again?"

The two children nod and go with us up the staircase. They look silently at Klärchen, who is lying just as she was when I saw her; they are seeing a dying person for the first time.

In the living room, coffee, rolls, and sausage have been set out. I eat mechanically and show prints of the photos that I took at the church fete.

Klärchen's sister sighs deeply and cries out mournfully as she looks at the pictures: "How quickly it happens, how quickly it happens: just think, it was only four weeks ago!"

In the picture that I give her, Klärchen is sitting and listening to Father with interest as he talks to her. He has his right hand at chest height, three fingers stretched out. His illness doesn't show. He looks much more lively than he usually did during his last months.

Klärchen's sister, who cannot come to the cemetery, urges us to leave: "You'd better go now—you must be there when your father is brought."

As we climb into the car we hear the church bells ringing for the first time. They reverberate through the stillness of the village. I feel a sinking in my stomach, gooseflesh spreading up my body, a tightness in my chest. I keep gasping for breath. That feeling of loneliness, welling up from my childhood. I have to beat down my tears.

It was like that often when I sat at my desk, staring out the window. Father had bought a television for me and put it into my room. "So that you don't go out so often with your friends but do your schoolwork," he said, after a visit to my teacher had once more darkened his face.

One day I found a note in his handwriting on top of my books: "The strong man is at his most powerful when alone" (Schiller). No other word. He had found out that I had a steady girlfriend.

On the way to the cemetery outside the village I overtake black-clad figures making their way singly or in groups to the burial. They emerge from all the side roads: we form a straggly procession.

"Behave yourselves well," I impress upon my daughters. "For your Grandpa Herman's sake, don't make comments or do anything silly."

Saying that is unnecessary, for all day long the two children are like robots, dumb and expressionless.

At the gate of the cemetery we meet the other close relatives. My sister is wearing sunglasses to hide the tears she expects to shed.

"Mother hasn't yet arrived," she says. "Horst has driven her to the shoemaker in the next village: she stumbled when she got out of the car and ripped the heel of her shoe."

The viewing room is already full of people. They stand pressed against the walls. I hear a whisper clearly as I pass them: "That must be Sigfrid."

The coffin is already resting on two trestles, behind my large wreath. I step up to the coffin, stroke it.

I wonder, Is his head at this end or his feet?

I have a desire to bend down and kiss the coffin, but I let it go, for such public gestures seem to me too mawkish.

I notice familiar faces, greet a few people. A seriously ill cousin of my father's has come; yesterday evening I was told she was too ill for the journey; she was sitting wrapped in a woolen blanket by a flickering coal stove.

"She's gone funny in the head and understands hardly anything," whispers her daughter to me. But she seems quite normal when I talk to her.

"I hope she doesn't give up the ghost here," I think to myself.

An elderly woman jumps up from her chair and clasps my hands.

"Ach Sigfrid, Sigfrid," she cries repeatedly, with tears in her eyes. "I've been so ill—I was in bed till this morning. Just think, I couldn't even order a wreath for your father, but I can send one later, my dear, can't I?"

When her only son died, twenty years ago, she and her husband had to look after the whole farm again on their own; they had wanted to retire, to hand the work over to their son and daughter-in-law. The woman is nearly eighty: they had kept the farm until her husband died a few years ago. She was always a nice, good woman, but I remember at this moment something that happened when the first refugees came to the village after the war.

In this big farmhouse, which had many empty rooms, a family with three children was to be quartered in two milkmaids' rooms over the cowsheds. Her husband was dead against this. I was there as a child when the horse cart with the refugees' furniture came. There was a big crowd in front of the farmhouse, and the farmer tried to strike the destitute refugees with an ax. The police constable and some burly men had to bind him with a cow chain to bring him under control.

— — —

I sit in the first row on the second chair, leaving the other free for my mother. The pastor appears and asks for our patience, for the organ is not yet working. It has to be dragged out of the neighboring room and pushed up close to the coffin. An assistant clears away some of the wreaths, throws one directly on top of mine.

I'm annoyed, for my wreath is now scarcely visible. People are still crowding into the room. I look toward the door, which is open slightly.

A sudden cramp in my heart: an illusion that Father has just walked in. One of the old men there has the same head and the same build and thin white hair as Father.

At last Mother arrives. She holds a bouquet of white lilies in her arms.

"Quite an adventure," she whispers. "The shoemaker—the only one for miles around—was sick in bed. We had to hammer on the door to get him up! Just bash a thick nail in, I said; the shoes only have to last for the burial."

The organ begins to play. During the sermon, I stare at the coffin almost unwaveringly. The pastor begins with a quotation from the Psalms: "The Lord is gracious, and full of compassion; slow to anger, and of great mercy. The Lord is good to all." And then he asks, "In the face of death, what value should we give to a career?"

While he speaks, he keeps looking at me. He mentions personal details, collected from me: speaks of Father's walk the day before he died, how he went to sleep and died peacefully. Behind the sound of the words I hear an indictment: not much understanding. But he does everything very decently—though almost inaudibly—and I hold nothing against him. I myself am still struggling to understand.

I walk behind the coffin—carried by four black-suited pallbearers—with my mother holding my arm. "This is the first time I have been in the first row behind a coffin," I think.

On the way I take the red roses I have brought out of their paper and share them with my wife and daughters. After the last prayer in front of the grave—in which my father now lies—the pastor comes up to us.

I introduce him to my mother, sister, and half brother. Suddenly, around me are four men who have laid a wreath in the name of the Reich Labor Service.

Father had been their first district doctor, after the service was founded in Westmark (the Nazi name for the Palatinate). He had always attended their fellowship meetings, and now they had a special request to make. They would like to set up a small museum: could I make available to them a few mementos from Father's belongings? His certificates of appointment, his uniform badges, his correspondence?

We agree that I should send them some copies. Father had played only a temporary role in the Reich Labor Service. He was responsible for all medical and hygienic facilities, helped enthusiastically with the building of the service, but quarreled very soon with the then Gauleiter of Westmark. The Gauleiter broke off Father's contract because of his "political unreliability" and refused to give him official status. Father protested against this without success.

In the parish hall the tables are already set, there is the smell of brewing coffee, and there are plates everywhere with crumble cakes and ring cakes. I am asked by the women who have organized all this whether the pastor has been invited.

"Doesn't he come anyway?" I ask.

"No," they say. I should go straight to the presbytery—he'll be offended otherwise.

A fat cat nuzzles against my legs as I stand in front of the presbytery, waiting until a window upstairs opens; it follows the pastor as we walk together to the parish hall. I thank him for the sermon, for his insight into our complicated situation; also for having spoken with such subtle pointedness.

"Those who have ears to hear, let them hear," he says. He listens as I tell him about our last visit to Aunt Klärchen.

"She's taken no fluid for several days," I say. "She can't have long to go. If her heart wasn't so strong and relaxed, she would have been dead long ago."

The pastor stands up, murmurs that he has something to see to, and leaves. Later I hear that he has said final prayers over Aunt Klärchen, and she dies that evening.

There are lively conversations going on round the tables. People keep changing places, going from one to another. Everywhere memories are exchanged. There are many people whom I'm meeting for the first time: offspring of Father's parents' siblings.

Now and then people talk of Father too.

Anecdotes are swapped about the days of his medical practice.

Mother's first encounter with Father was in the doctor's waiting room. She heard the old women there talking about him.

"Straight as a gun barrel!" one of them said. "One can see that he was in the army for a long time. One day my sister goes into his consulting room and says: 'Herr Doctor, I can hardly walk anymore. Can you have a look at my feet? What can I do about them?'

"Then the doctor mutters something about a remedy and gives her a prescription. She takes it to the pharmacist's, thinking, 'Who cares what it is? Maybe it will help.' The pharmacist reads the prescription, and just grins and tells her that he can't give it to her now: the front tires are flat.

"'What can't you give me?' asks my sister in disbelief. 'The doctor has prescribed something for me, because I can't walk anymore.'

"'Quite,' says the chemist. 'He's prescribed you a bicycle.'"

Mother was bursting with laughter as she listened to this, but the two women were quite serious.

"He jokes with people in this way," they said.

"It was the same with our neighbor," the other woman said.

"She was suffering from unbearable headaches; she went to his office and said, 'My headaches are becoming unbearable. I'll have to hang myself.' He gave her a prescription too, but no one except the chemist could read his handwriting. She went to the pharmacist's. The prescription said: 'A rope to hang herself.'"

"Father later confirmed these funny stories," said Mother. "They were women who had pretended to be ill to get their pensions earlier."

But I also hear about other things: how he had diagnosed at a glance a brain infection in a young boy who had been treated for several days as if he had flu—and thus saved his life at the last minute; how he had cadged some penicillin from an American military hospital, as it was not in stock at the German hospital.

I hear that in the last days of the war he protected more than a hundred soldiers from imprisonment—men who happened to be in Einöllen during the German retreat. Before the American tanks arrived the following day, the women of the village cut up sheets and swastika flags and sewed Red Cross arm bands out of them. By flying a big Red Cross flag from the schoolhouse, Father had passed the village off as a military hospital, and the soldiers—who were now all going around with arm bands—as orderlies. He had himself been in Einöllen by chance, treating a man with a bullet in his chest; American low fliers had shot at the man while he was en route to the Luftwaffe hospital at Meisenheim—in a Red Cross jeep that was clearly marked as such. Father operated in the school on him and on other wounded soldiers, including one who had seven machine-gun bullets in him.

I hear how he was incorruptible. Farmers would slip him eggs, meat, and fruit to try to bribe him into issuing false medical certificates to get their sons out of military service. Although we ourselves didn't have enough to eat, Father gave the food to those who were genuinely sick.

I hear how he was unyielding. One day a poor man—who already had seven children—asked him to perform an abortion on his wife. "I'll pay you well," the man had said and had put a mark on the table—a lot of money, just after the war. But the wife bled to death at the hands of a backstreet abortionist.

I hear how he stitched up—without anesthetic—the tongue of a young man who in a drunken brawl had bitten half his tongue off. "To teach him a lesson," he said, for Father never drank alcohol; but maybe it was because it would have been dangerous to give a narcotic to someone with so much alcohol in his bloodstream.

"One can say what one likes, but the man certainly stood out." This is said by my cousin Karl—whose father and grandfather were called Karl, and whose son is Karl too. He looks through the last pictures that I took of Father.

The cold air outside the parish hall carries the same village smells that accompanied my childhood. I notice this without interest. The voices of the guests at the gathering for my dead father seem to come from a great distance.

# VIII

You were a good doctor, someone said, a superb diagnostician. You recognized the illness at a glance, ordered the right treatment after two or three other doctors had already struggled in vain.

"Stiff as a gun barrel," said another: unapproachable and unfriendly. "I've got such pains in my legs," your sister complained, "bad varicose veins. What can I do?"

"Amputate them," you said.

"Our son has such an awful cold, Herr Doctor," some acquaintances had said. "He's been sneezing and coughing dreadfully for three weeks. What can be done about it?"

"Nothing," you said.

True, a cold lasts just as long with medical treatment as without. But other doctors would have prescribed harmless palliatives to reassure the relatives; they would have made several home visits, and made money from them.

You said "Nothing," but at the same time explained exactly how the patient should be nursed, asking for no fee. You took three marks for a home visit during the day and five marks for a night visit, when others took ten times as much. And for most of the farmers, your fees remained "money owing."

You got your money only if we got our hair cut by the barber who was one of your patients and we said, "Father will settle it."

Or if I fetched bread from the baker who was another of your patients and I said, "Father will settle it."

You got your officer's pension, and it was only pro forma that you
were registered by the medical council as a specialist in internal
diseases. You were not allowed to work as a state-paid doctor. It
was not forgotten that you had a past.

You were in bed by eight o'clock every evening. You lay awake and
scratched your head. For hours on end—so it seemed to me—I
heard the monotonous scraping of fingernails over your scalp and
hair: slow—SCRAPE, slow—SCRAPE: first slowly over the
whole head, then suddenly scratching over your crown to your
ear. Slow—SCRAPE, slow—SCRAPE. There might be voices
outside the window—or a knocking on the door or window. You
remained lying there, but after a while you would say to me, "Go
to the window and ask what they want."

"Our Helmut has had a heart attack: could your father come
at once?"

"They're asking if you can come," I would say. "Someone has
had a heart attack."

"Ask who it is," you replied.

I passed the question out through the window.

I relayed the reply back inside.

"I get soaked with sweat if I get up at this time; I catch cold.
Tell them that."

I rephrased this, toned it down.

"I think it really is urgent," I said to you then.

You growled and told me to tell them that you would come.

"He's just totally sozzled again," you said, although you knew
that this young man had a minor heart murmur. But you also knew
that he liked drinking and these attacks came only when he was
drunk.

And tonight the pub opposite would be a riot: Saturday evening.

I went back to bed and listened—from under the bedclothes—to you getting dressed. The bedroom in the old farmhouse had no cellar beneath and was unheated. The thick featherbeds were ice cold in winter, and one had to use a hot-water bottle. You got into bed with your underwear on: a long-sleeved undershirt, long underpants, wooly socks. Only when the featherbed had to some extent warmed up did you begin to undress. First, the socks; then—perhaps a quarter of an hour later—the long underpants. Then, after another quarter of an hour, the undershirt. You slept naked; night after night you were truly soaked with sweat. And a night visit like this could bring on another attack of asthma.

I felt ashamed nonetheless that people always had to beg before you would come.

You got fully dressed in front of your bed and then went over to your consulting room. Your desk was there and a bookshelf with manuscripts and books on racial research. You kept your medical equipment in an old wooden cabinet: samples from pharmaceutical firms, the device for measuring blood pressure, bandages, wadding; and in other compartments, hammer and pliers, nails, string, riding spurs, various uniform belts. Your grandmother's worm-eaten spinning wheel stood on top of the cabinet.

In a glass-fronted cabinet there were dozens of tweezers and clips and pairs of scissors of all shapes and sizes, together with adhesive tape and a syringe and some needles in a metal box.

For this house visit you selected an ampoule, put the metal box with the syringe in your trouser pocket, and stuck the sphygmomanometer for measuring blood pressure under your arm. You also had ether and wadding in your jacket pocket. When you made a home visit, you insisted first of all on some boiling water to sterilize the syringe. You used needles dozens of times, even when they had become quite blunt. You went on using and sterilizing this syringe long after disposable plastic syringes had become available.

Together with a tiny stump of a pencil and a bent-open paper clip—with which you could clean your fingernails for hours on end (or so I imagined)—you always had in your jacket pocket a tiny metal saw. You used it for lots of things, and also when you made that home visit—to cut open the injection ampoule.

I often sat on the couch in your consulting room, which was set apart for medical examinations and was covered with a white cloth—graying and unchanged for years. This couch—the only other piece of furniture in the consulting room beyond what I have already mentioned—was actually an old trunk. Your father had stored his meager possessions in it on voyages to America and Africa. After his death, it came back to his parental home. When you were not there, I used to rummage in it secretly. It was packed with books and journals. The collected works of Lanz von Lieben-fels, for example, and journals about runes, and author's copies of your own books: *New Foundations for Racial Research, The Faith of the Germans, The Ancient German Constitution, Calendar and Custom.*

I didn't know when you returned home that night—I was asleep. But I think it must have been at about nine o'clock. I could only guess how early you normally went to sleep. On some evenings I would hear on the radio a satirical program from Berlin—and it was the first time I heard anything about politics, which to my knowledge were never discussed at home. These programs began at eight o'clock, and you were already in bed—immediately after the evening news.

As a doctor, you were incorruptible, but you did get involved in one illegal situation. There was a young woman in the village who had been lying in bed, incurably ill, for years. Her whole body was a single septic sore. She often screamed so loudly with pain that the whole neighborhood could hear her. The doctors had stopped treating her: morphine gave her relief, but its supply was strictly controlled; it could not be used on a permanent basis. The old mother of this woman kept coming to you in tears, imploring you to inject her daughter with morphine.

"Help her, help her, Herr Doctor, " she wailed. "The poor thing can't bear it anymore, and I can't bear it either, Herr Doctor." She slipped you eggs and meat and sausage. Now and then, when you could give a patient morphine with a clear conscience, you ordered extra from the pharmacist and gave it to the young woman.

She injected it herself, and for one ampoule she paid you four times more than it had cost.

In the course of time, you gradually let yourself get drawn in.

You bought morphine in the names of various patients, and then sold ampoule after ampoule to the old woman. You did this reluctantly, but you got sucked in.

Sometimes I had to deliver the ampoules for you. I would see the young woman lying on her back in a sparkling white bed: the bed was so perfectly made, it looked as if it was unused—no creases in the sheets or coverlet. The young woman lay with yellowy white cheeks; her blond hair was like a crown round her head; her hands lay limp on the coverlet.

Like a corpse, I thought.

She groaned softly.

I handed over the ampoule (always just one), took the five-mark note, and made my way home.

I knew that the whole thing was not quite aboveboard.

I pieced the true situation together from what you said and from the old woman's bellyaching.

One day the pharmacist in Lauterecken reported you. He had noticed the amount of morphine that you supposedly used in your small village. He suspected that you were yourself addicted to morphine, and the medical council set up an investigation.

But you produced prescriptions only in the names of patients whom you had actually injected with morphine.

The trade between you and the old woman ceased. I think that I noticed then that you were at the time grateful for these extra earnings. When I went to the old woman for the last time—with a packet of three or four ampoules—she took it hesitantly. Pressing the money into my hand, she said, "Tell your father that we don't need any more now."

You nodded when I told you. I have often asked myself how well this squared with your reputation for incorruptibility.

I knew that you had slid into it. I still have the wailing, complaining, and begging of the old woman clear in my memory. She was related to you besides.

You were a good doctor, someone said. Others knew how— when you had your office close to the Devil's Moor—ten patients would be sitting in the waiting room before you could be persuaded at last to get up.

"They can wait," you said.

# 9

I take a stroll with Uwe through the village, as far as the cemetery. Uwe is my female cousin's son; he has just passed his *Abitur* and in a few days' time must start his community service in a home for children with learning disabilities. I tell him about my student days, about my own work as a teacher of children with learning disabilities and difficulties.

"Military service would have been impossible for me to avoid," I say. "I couldn't have let Father down."

"No one becomes a man until he is a lieutenant," he would sometimes say—grinning, but he truly meant it. He was proud of being able to strut around—in the uniform of a lieutenant colonel—the village where as a boy he had to herd cattle along to the fields.

I did indeed complete my service, becoming a lieutenant in the reserve. It was a hard time for me, for this kind of dealing with subordinates was at odds with all my pedagogical principles. But I've never learned so much about people as I did during that time.

Things that Father in his day had reveled in were excruciating to me: such as when someone late at night in the officers' mess would bawl out the young soldiers with barrack-room coarseness.

We walk past the houses in which I used to play as a child. There are lights still on in the cowsheds; a farmer forks manure onto the pile in front of the house; it steams in the cold air. At one time, Father had carried out that task.

"Father was born in this house," I say, as we pass the open square in the middle of the village. And now he lies up there in the cemetery, in a wooden box, icy cold, and beginning to rot. Strange that yesterday I saw him for the last time in my life.

The Woll sisters live there: I show Uwe the house and tell him about my meeting yesterday with the two women in their shop.

As a city boy, he knows about such shops only from nostalgic TV programs about "Aunty Emma Shops."

"It's an odd feeling to have a father like him," I say. "You wouldn't comprehend it, Uwe—which is just as well."

When I was in the top grade at school, we saw a film. It reported how—by an order from Himmler—children from Polish families who were blond and blue eyed were taken from their relatives and brought to Germany to be brought up as future leaders in Napola schools. None of those who saw the film knew that this idea emanated from my father. He photographed some of these children during the war when he was with Antiaircraft Regiment 17 in East Poland, sent Himmler the photos, and suggested that this kind of German stock should be rescued from pernicious Slavic influence. The transportation program stemmed from that.

The film had upset me greatly. As we emerged from it, I spoke about it to a Franciscan nun who had a doctorate in German and who had also seen the film with her class. But she hardly listened, kept looking at her watch, murmured that she must get to the chapel quickly for prayers. Yet she was one of the few adults with whom, at that time, I could really converse.

Uwe responds little, asks only brief questions, but he understands well that I have a right to soliloquize, that I want to organize my thoughts rather than actually discuss this whirling mixture of experiences and feelings, memories and reflections, buffeting me with positive and negative emotions.

I have recently found a card in Father's bookcase—one that he wrote to his mother when he was fourteen. His handwriting was immediately recognizable; it had scarcely altered at all in the subsequent sixty-five years.

Just as Father himself had not altered.

As a schoolboy he had published poems in newspapers which he might easily have written in the last year of his life. He had fought unremittingly for his idea of a German Reich and had unremittingly lost the fight: fought for a seemingly perfect world in which all people would have the same rights, in which no one would be allowed to sell off anyone else's property by force, in which no one would be forced into exile in order to earn enough to support his family and then be ruined.

I decide that it was the shock of his father's death—for which he blamed the Jews of Amsterdam who had allegedly swindled him—and then the poverty and suffering into which his mother was plunged that had fixed the course of his life.

He depended greatly on her and saw how greatly she had to overwork, how despite all her efforts the family did not prosper.

But then I immediately think of counterarguments and find my search for an explanation lame. Herbert, I reflect, would have asked whether it was better to be swindled by non-Jews; or whether Jews might not also be swindled and sometimes not only that; or whether a single swindle gave one a pretext for genocide; or whether the swindle had actually been proved, whether it might actually have been no more than a misconception of the facts. "Your grandfather was just as unprepossessing in appearance as your father," Herbert would have said. "They both tried to blame their misfortunes on other, more fortunate people."

"For Heaven's sake, Uwe," I say out loud, "I know my own schizophrenic situation only too well: to love my father as a person but to be horrified by his personality."

We go past the last houses in the village, past shops that are already closed. It is cold. The sky is cloudless, and the contours of the hills and meadows, and the silhouette of the village itself, might seem romantic. But I have no feelings toward this village. Never in the last few years have I had the wish to visit it again, to walk along the roads where I played as a child. It is dead to me.

"Father always tried," I say to the silent Uwe, "to influence my life along his own lines, kept rolling stones along the road for me—with the best intention, so he believed.

"He hardly exchanged a word with my wife because she had brown eyes and dark hair; and he took little notice of my children because they were not—as he wished—called Sigrun and Swanhild, but Susanne and Elisabeth."

"Perhaps he took it hard that you were so against him?" asked Uwe.

"But that was not the case," I answered. "True, I went my own way, followed it through despite his disapproval, but I was always there when he needed me—and he did need me often. I could not in fact think evil of him: I believed I understood his situation, had sympathy for him.

"One day—when I was about twelve years old—I found a note in his bookcase on which he had written, 'Should I become a child killer?' Two days later it was no longer there, but I was frightened out of my wits.

"I don't know what he was planning: whether he was thinking of himself and all of us because life in this day and age seemed senseless to him, whether this was an aftereffect of his war experience. I never asked him about it.

"He could do very irrational, very horrible things, of which I prefer not to talk, and then make quite touching gestures.

"By chance I came across a thank-you letter a little while ago. It was apparent from it that he had supported a family over many years with gifts of money. The husband was incapable of working: a failure who was constantly sunk in debt but who had a large family to support. Father virtually paid for the studies of his sons, who are all in good positions today. He really had to scrimp and save to do that. And why? Because in his own youth he had much to be grateful for to the father of this man."

We enter the cemetery. The grave has been heaped up with earth; the piled-up wreaths glimmer in the darkness. Right at the front I see my own wreath with the three hundred yellow roses. I stand before the grave in which my father lies and wonder what inner reactions I should actually feel. Grief? Pain?

I observe the grave like a photograph, consider from which angle—and with what objective—I might photograph it over the next few days.

This act of standing at the grave seems so stupid to me. Whom does it serve? Father knows nothing of it. I have no thoughts such as: I shall see you again in the next world.

"By the way," I say to Uwe, "your grandfather's name is carved here." I turn away from the grave, toward the war memorial that was erected only a few weeks ago. "Your great-grandmother and her mother lie under the memorial, and a further seven generations of our ancestors are in this graveyard. But they don't mean anything to you."

"Perhaps they will later," says Uwe; but I don't believe him.

*IX*

"Can you tell me," you often asked in your last months, "what the meaning of life is?"

I couldn't give you an answer.

I thought, After eight decades, you still don't know.

You also asked Mother this question.

"Life itself is the meaning of life," answered Mother.

A good answer, I thought, but you were not satisfied with it.

The atrophy of your optical nerve sent you almost crazy with fear—fear that you would go blind.

"I can hardly read anymore," you said. "I can no longer write. When I want to read a book, I need a magnifying glass; I see just part of the line and have to piece it together word by word. And I can't write articles anymore."

It was particularly bad on the days when you suffered from a lack of oxygen. You were bad tempered and would harass everyone in the house.

After your stomach operation you could no longer eat cold food. You would dip a sausage into tea to warm it up.

You looked at your watch and said, "I need to eat again." You would time your meals to the minute to keep your senile diabetes under control. You calculated your carbohydrate requirements exactly.

Whoever was there had to drop whatever he or she was doing to prepare your meal immediately.

When it was served to you, you would be sitting up but already asleep again from weakness.

"Here's your food," you'd be told. "Eat it up before it gets cold."

You would look up briefly, with cloudy, glassy eyes that were turning bluish red round the irises, and then fall asleep again.

Then you would wake again and call out that your food was cold.

It would be heated up again for you.

"The tea is too hot and the sausage is too cold," you said, after testing them suspiciously.

They would be heated to the right temperature again, and then you would fall asleep over them.


Your condition altered with the weather.

You would suddenly be able to breathe better and would no longer have to sleep all day long in your typical posture—sitting up, with your head resting on your arm to maximize oxygen intake into the fraction of your lungs that was still functioning. You ordered a taxi and waited outside the door for it; even in fine weather you had a sturdy umbrella with you to lean on.

You were too proud to use a stick.

"It's unsoldierly," you said.

There were two pictures of you in a frame above your desk, with an inscription beneath in Gothic script: "Soldiers are always soldiers; one sees that with every step. . . ."

You would direct the taxi to the café. On one such outing the taxi driver caused an accident: your face hit the windshield and was quite badly cut.

The shock and annoyance of this made your illness worse again.

You refused to be a witness for the prosecution or to accept compensation from the taxi driver's insurance.

"One shouldn't do that," you said. "The taxi driver didn't do it on purpose."

Similarly, you didn't report an incident when a drunken soccer fan returning from a soccer match hurled an empty beer bottle at an approaching bus that you were in: the bottle smashed through the window and hit you in the face. Your eyes were injured: you groped along the edge of the road to the first house in the next village and asked for help. You needed treatment for a whole year: the tear ducts had to be cleared repeatedly—there were tears constantly rolling down your cheeks or through your nostrils.

The perpetrator suffered no consequences at all for his act of high spirits. After the police had identified him, they asked you to file a complaint. You refused. The man came to apologize to you. He took an unpaid day off especially to do so. "People don't do that," you said, "if they are reported. The man is working class, he has a big family to support, and he didn't do it on purpose."

On the other hand, you brought many pointless legal cases against people who had annoyed you, who you believed deliberately wished to harm you.

You also took taxis out into the woods. The increased oxygen there enabled you to breathe better, you said. The taxi driver waited by the edge of the road, while you walked up and down.

Soldiers are always soldiers; one sees that with every step. . . .

You asked me for the meaning of life.

At six years old I would have answered, "A wristwatch with an expandable metal band and a pair of skiing boots."

I would lie awake in bed at that time and picture to myself what it would feel like to stick a knife into a boy in the village who flaunted those unattainable treasures and took them for granted: how I would pull the boots off him and slip on the wristwatch.

———

At twelve years old I would have answered, "Trousers without patches and shoes without holes." At the boarding school I was the only pupil who was allowed to wear short trousers on the first sunny—but still chilly—day of spring: the houseparent couldn't find a wearable pair of long trousers in my wardrobe, even though he fought determinedly through the clutter that he found there. (No one had ever taught me how to keep things tidy.)

As a fifteen-year-old I would have answered, "To have a father who has enough money to buy groceries." "Now we can be counted among the rich," you said when you exchanged your old, rusty VW for a new one. "We must tighten our belts," you said. "The car was very expensive."

You cut out our daily visits to the café together.

We went around your acquaintances in turn in pursuit of afternoon coffee.

They made coffee, laid rolls or cakes before us, and made a great effort to keep up the conversation.

You also made an effort, but after a few sentences you dried up, and we all lapsed into silence. We sat there for exactly two hours, until you looked at your watch and took leave.

I still remember the afternoon when we turned up at the home of a family who exactly one week ago had been our hosts.

You rang the bell and we climbed the stairs. On the upper landing the lady of the house was standing with a cleaning rag and a jug of water. She bent down over the sparkling clean stairs and hunted for some more dust.

"I'm afraid I can't ask you in today, Herr Doctor," she said. "We're cleaning the house."

You nodded, said good-bye, and descended the stairs again. I crept along behind you. "They don't want us anymore," you said when we got outside the door. "We've been there too often." And you looked at me, raised your eyebrows, and adopted your typical demeanor—half ironic, half ashamed.

As a seventeen-year-old I would have answered, "To have my own room, books, some changes of clothes." Maybe you would have given me money for those if I had pleaded for it. But I thought you would then be short of food again, so I let it rest. I began to write at that time for the local newspaper. Every evening I sat in the lecture hall of the adult education school and made notes: on the beauty of the Greek Islands, on Germany's role in world politics, on the romanticism and reality of the circus. With the money I earned I bought books, jeans, and a pullover.

Perhaps I should have asked you in return: about the meaning of life for the young Anne Frank, for example; about the meaning of life for the parents, siblings, and relatives of my London friends, with whose daughters your granddaughter corresponded so naturally on topics such as the Beatles, fashion, travel; about the meaning of life for Ludwig Moses from Kusel, whose investigations you managed to wriggle out of at the denazification hearing. You kept a newspaper clipping: Ludwig Moses had died soon after the hearing from all that he had suffered in the concentration camp. He was the only survivor from his family.

As a young man you had sought the meaning of life in the Icelandic sagas; in 1934 you were sent by Darré on a government visit to Iceland, and as an old man you underlined sayings from the Elder Edda in pencil.

"One should not be boastful" had been underlined in that ancient poem the "Hávamál." You kept telling the story of how when you had your civilian job with the Reich, you drove one of your friends to the home of some acquaintances of his in your smart new cabriolet. When he got out, your friend said proudly to his hosts, "This is my driver." They misconstrued this and asked you to wait for your friend in the servants' kitchen. When they sat down to eat, your absence was suddenly noticed. The red faces, the embarrassment, the thousandfold apologies were vivid in your memory thirty years later.

"No more valuable load can be carried on the road than a strong intelligence; one takes no worse supply for the journey than an excess of ale." You never drank alcohol, "because drink reveals a side of one's character one would prefer to control."

Similarly underlined by you: "The glutton, if he is not careful, eats himself sick." Most of the tests that you asked to be sent to you after stays in the hospital indicated considerable malnutrition. After the burst stomach ulcer—which you only just survived—you had only a quarter of your stomach left. That suited you, for you now had an excuse to eat even less.

"If you suffer harm, do harm in return; don't make peace with the enemy!" You collected a thick packet of cuttings over the years concerning deception, fraud, bankruptcy. You underlined the names of those mentioned in red: those whose first names were David or Moses or Samuel. The surnames stemmed from the nineteenth century, when a new law forced them to take them: Rosenblatt or Veilchenduft or Grünstein. And there were conspicuous exclamation marks and thick underlinings when diamonds were mentioned, or Amsterdam.

"I saw how a woman's false word cost a man his head: treacherous tongues and untrue accusations brought him to his death." Brown eyes lie, you said to me once. You always admired blue-eyed girls. You always tried to impress them.

As a boy you made—from instructions in a physics book—a machine that gave light electrical shocks if one held its two metal handles. You took pleasure in getting a girl from the village to take hold of the handles. Your mother gave you a terrific scolding when she heard the screams of the girl in your room.

When you were a successful officer from Berlin, reputed in the village to be Himmler's personal physician, you invited the belles of Einöllen for an evening ride in your new car. You showed them your best side, talked, joked; at that time there were no halogen headlights and no streetlights outside the village. You failed to see the curb and drove straight over it. The car came to a halt right at the edge of the stream and slowly turned over onto its side. The girls had to climb out of the car through the side windows, and a farmer's team of oxen pulled the car up onto the road again.

One can see this as a metaphor for your relationship with women. You would worship a girl for her Germanic good looks, and then—when you discovered that a Valkyrie could have flaws and weaknesses like any other person—you would condemn her according to your racial theories. You would suddenly notice non-Nordic characteristics in her: a non-Aryan brow, a negroid pelvis, a sharp kink in the knee joints as in the Neanderthals.

"Property dies, clans die, you yourself die too; I only know one thing that lasts: the fame of heroic deeds." The Elder Edda ends with those verses. You constantly quoted them.

Your military decorations were displayed next to *Who's Who in Germany* and Kürschner's *Directory of German Scholars*. You said to me once, "Officers of the Wehrmacht too can be buried with military honors on application to the Bundeswehr."

You asked me about the meaning of life. I didn't answer, but asked you in return if you were frightened of death. You denied that you were, but you took your meals on the dot, made sure you had your injections at the prescribed time, and calculated your diet down to the last calorie: did everything, in fact, to prolong your life.

It was a miracle you had lived so long, the doctor treating you said to me. He didn't think you would last another winter. You lasted several more winters.

On the way back from the burial my daughter said to me sternly, "Daddy, I want to say something, but promise that you won't be cross."

"What is it, Susanne?" I asked.

"I think," she said, "that you actually feel nothing for your father. You were the only one who wasn't crying."

127

# *10*

A section of the guests—the children of Father's brothers—come in my car to the house where my sister and mother live. The loosely strung-out column of vehicles—whose makes and dimensions are calling cards for the professional standing of their drivers—closes up as it passes the site of an accident.

"Like the day before yesterday," I recall, "when I set out after receiving my mother's telephone call."

But this time I just see dented metal and angry but unblemished faces.

We park in front of the large, nineteenth-century villa that my sister and brother-in-law bought some years ago. They live on the upper floor, my parents on the ground floor. My father's bedroom has a door with two panels of glass, romanesque in style.

"Synagogue windows," my father said once. "The man who built the house was a Jew. And this is the room where he died. It is a punishment for me that I must spend my last days in this room."

"The shape of the panels may be a coincidence," I said, but he insisted. And he did die in this room.

My sister's flat is furnished like something out of *House Beautiful*. Antique furniture, but on the walls, modern graphics, rifles, bayonets, and some of Father's things. I leave the circle of conversation—which touches not at all on the events of the last few days, or even of today—and go into Father's room. I think about the amazing changes in him during his last years. Earlier, he had scrimped and saved without letup, never got into debt. He bought a new suit only when the old one could no longer be patched, and then, if possible, only on sale or secondhand. Just as the money he worked for when he was a student was reduced by inflation to the value of a bus ticket, so his savings at the end of the Second World War also lost their worth. They remained rolled up in a storage jar in his medicine cabinet, labeled "Poison." He had wanted to buy a farmhouse with them, but after the currency reform we children used them for games.

But during his last years he let his hair grow down to his neck, whereas before it had always been cropped to military shortness. He ordered made-to-measure suits, and he began to travel. He went for the first time to the Frankfurt Book Fair, at which two of his books were exhibited. He was in high spirits there and withstood the stress of it without an attack of asthma.

"I should have done that long ago," he said to me, "sought direct contact with people. I always just corresponded with my publishers, never got to know them personally."

He went on trips by air to Majorca and the Canary Islands.

"I've stopped feeling bored and fed up with myself," he wrote from Tenerife. "Today the excursions began. We went by bus to the top of the 3,700-meter-high volcano Teyde. The journey up was sunny, and the change in altitude didn't bother me at all; but then, in addition to the already existing snow and ice, hail and mist came down, and we drove through clouds for an hour on the way down—and that brought on some asthma. We are going on an air trip to Morocco tomorrow, if there are still some seats left."

Father told me that on the flight to Tenerife he had sent word to the pilot that he had been an officer with the Luftwaffe. He was then invited into the cockpit. On the island he wore his old white Luftwaffe uniform—without stripes, of course. He bought white shoes for himself, and everyone treated him most courteously.

This was a Father that I didn't know. I was reminded of Brecht's story "The Disreputable Old Lady," but in contrast to her there was an absence in his life again afterward. His euphoria was followed by setbacks and personal disappointments. He withdrew to his bed, in which even twenty or thirty years ago he used to lie until midday, gazing at the bedspread, slowly scratching his scalp with his fingernails.

Now I am sitting on his bed, in the room where he died.

I pull open the drawer, in which his spectacles, syringe, and medications are still lying. I take in my hand the small inhaler that he would use when attacked by asthma, and puff it a little. I open the closet and take out his shoes, then put them back. I bend my head forward, into the closet, smell his suits. That was how Father smelled, I think; I try to take everything in precisely.

Mother comes into the room. "What are you looking for?" she asks.

"Nothing," I say. "I'm taking leave of my father."

I think again of Herbert, who often intentionally hurt me in our conversations over lager in pubs in Hampstead. How would he have reacted? Perhaps he would have said, "Unlike you, I can be proud of my dead father, whom I clung to as you did to yours." And also, "I didn't need three hundred yellow roses." And then he would have said once more, *"Free yourself of him."*

# Translator's Notes

page 6
**Abitur**
The school-leaving or graduation exam in the German high school system.

page 8
**Abiturient**
As an *Abiturient* (one who has passed his *Abitur*), he should have been able to calculate.

page 11
**Volkssturm**
The Nazis' final call-up, in September 1944. All able-bodied boys and men between the ages of sixteen and sixty were included.

page 16
**gymnasium**
The boarding school was attached to a gymnasium. Sigfrid was sent there because his parents had separated.

page 29
**Palatinate**
The Rhineland state (Pfalz) that was incorporated in 1946 into the state of Rheinland-Pfalz. The name was originally given to all the imperial castles where the Holy Roman emperor stayed on his journeys through Germany, but it became identified from about the eleventh century on with territory on both sides of the river held

by the Count Palatine of the Rhine. The French, under Napoleon and in World Wars I and II, occupied the area.

page 40
## Hofbräuhaus in Munich
Historic tavern, dating from the sixteenth century, in which Hitler held many meetings in the 1920s.

page 41
### separatists
Between 1918 and 1930 the west side of the Rhine was occupied by the French. The separatists wanted to detach the Palatinate (Pfalz) from Germany and turn it into an autonomous republic.

page 46
## Reich Labor Service
*Reichsarbeitdienst*. From 1935, all men and women between the ages of eighteen and twenty-five had to do six months of unpaid physical labor: harvesting for the women, highway building for the men, and the like.

page 49
## German Faith Movement
*Deutsche Glaubensbewebung*. A religious organization with a National Socialist ideology.

page 51
### blood orders
Hitler created these honors after the unsuccessful Putsch of 8 and 9 November 1923. The Bavarian government ordered the police to fire on Nazi demonstrators. The casualties became members of the *Blutorden*.

page 52
## NSDAP
*Nationalsozialistische Deutsche Arbeiter-Partei* (National Socialist German Workers Party). The Nazi party.

page 67
**RFSS**
*Reichsführung SS.* Heinrich Himmler's ministry.

page 74
***Realgymnasium***
A gymnasium specializing in natural science, as opposed to a classical (Latin- and Greek-based) gymnasium.

page 85
**ZDF**
*Zweites Deutsches Fernsehen.* German television's channel 2.

page 88
**aid program for citizens of the Rhine-Ruhr**
Under this program, the German government found jobs for German professionals who had lost their jobs in the French-occupied areas.

page 105
**The Lord is gracious . . . good to all**
Psalms 145:8–9.

page 117
**Napola schools**
Short for *Nationalpolitische Erziehungs-Anstalten.* Schools in which a selected elite were indoctrinated with Nazi ideas. Himmler advocated the transportation program as early as November 1939, so it is unlikely that the idea emanated from Gauch alone.

page 130
**"The Disreputable Old Lady"**
"Die unwürdige Greisin" (1939), first published in *Kalendergeschichten* (Berlin, 1949). It tells of an elderly widow who shocks her conventional children and relatives by suddenly living it up after years of self-denial.

## About the Author

Sigfrid Gauch was born in 1945 in Offenbach, Germany. His other books include *Goethes Foto, Zweiter Hand,* and *Winterhafen.* He lives in Mainz, Germany, where he is the director of the literature department of the Ministry of Culture.